For the Record …
Celebrating Piccadilly Radio
on its Fiftieth Anniversary 1974-2024
Brian Beech and Tony Ingham
ISBN: 978-1-914933-60-8

SPECIAL PRE-RELEASE EDITION

The rights of Brian Beech and Tony Ingham to be identified as the authors of this work has been asserted in accordance with the Copyright Designs and Patents Act 1988.

A copy of this book is deposited with the British Library.

Published By: -

i2i
PUBLISHING

i2i Publishing. Manchester.
www.i2i.publishing.co.uk

Foreword

Philip T. Birch, the founding
managing director of Piccadilly Radio

I became involved in what would become Piccadilly Radio
against the backdrop of growing concern in the industry for the
future of independent radio. Two independent radio stations in
London were experiencing significant financial difficulties,
which risked impacting the progress of independent radio.

Around this time, in 1973, I was contacted by a consortium
which called itself Greater Manchester Independent Radio
(GMIR) and asked to be its managing director. To my surprise,
the offer was followed by a call from John Thompson, Head of

Radio for the Independent Broadcasting Authority (IBA), urging me to accept. As Mr. Thompson explained, if big stations in London couldn't survive, who would risk investing in other, smaller stations? Mr. Thompson needed GMIR to triumph and given the 'huge successes' of my previous station, Radio London, he believed I was the person for the job. I was not immune to the flattery, but I would have accepted the job regardless.

The first challenge was locating a home for the future radio station and building its studios. I scoured central Manchester with the help of several other directors, and we finally found the perfect location - Piccadilly Plaza. After some heavy bargaining, we signed the lease.

The next step was gathering my team. To my delight, Lord Sidney Bernstein, Chairman of Granada Television, which was a shareholder of GMIR, took a personal interest in our project. He let us use the services of Granada's chief engineer, Geoffrey White, to build the studios. I discovered quickly that Geoff was one of the finest engineers in the country. His work was flawless, and he completed the project meticulously, despite the challenges the economy was facing at the time.

I had engaged a recent university graduate already, Jim Hancock, to act as a liaison on the days I was unable to be in Manchester. Jim had been the head of Manchester University's student union and had his finger on the pulse of the community. His youthful enthusiasm quickly endeared him to my team.

One of my main concerns was finding key staff members with the right experience. I knew if I chose right, they would be the heart and soul of the station. It soon became apparent, however, that I needn't have worried about finding the right people. They found me.

The first was Shiona Nelson Hawkins, who had a quick wit and a tireless work ethic. She had spent some time in America and had worked in the traffic department of Chicago's largest radio station. At the time, traffic departments of radio stations were responsible for collecting, screening, and scheduling commercials. I was impressed by her experience and hired her as my temporary assistant, with the understanding that once I collected my team, she would be responsible for setting up the traffic department and become its manager. (On a personal note, while I did not know it at the time, several years later, I would marry Shiona and as I write this, we have now been happily married for forty-two years.)

Soon after that, I received a letter from a man named Colin St. John Walters, who at the time was the manager of BBC Radio Nottingham. Colin was eager to get into commercial radio as a programme controller, so we agreed to meet. At first, I was concerned that Colin might be too immersed in BBC's formulaic style to be the creative and imaginative programme controller that commercial radio needed. I soon discovered, however, that he had spent significant time studying commercial radio and was ready for the role. I offered him the position and he accepted without hesitation. I suggested that he consider dropping St. John from his professional name and become just plain Colin Walters, which he did.

At about this time, I set myself one very important task: to come up with a fresh name for the station and push GMIR, an anagram for Grim, well into the background. I came up with the name 'Piccadilly Radio'. I liked the name because it would remind people of our location and it had a happy sound. Local advertisers would like it due to its connection with Manchester's Piccadilly Plaza and London advertisers would remember it because, in a light-hearted way, they regard their own Piccadilly Circus as the centre of the universe. Most important of all, our listeners would love it.

So, PICCADILLY RADIO it became.

The next applicant was Richard Bliss, a man who had experience selling newspaper advertising space and television airtime, and now wanted to get into radio as a sales manager. He arrived at my office carrying a large yellow legal pad, which he used to make copious notes throughout the interview. I was impressed. During our interview, very quickly, it became obvious that he would have no difficulty transitioning into radio. He settled in rapidly and to my surprise began selling advertising airtime almost immediately. I never saw him take notes again.

Piccadilly Radio also needed a promotions manager to be responsible for organising outside broadcasts, publicity events, and generally getting our name out there. We were lucky to land Tony Ingham, who became known as the best in the business and is the co-author of this book.

As we headed towards launch, myself and the team I had gathered were extremely busy interviewing potential staff to ensure we had a full complement before we aired. The task was massive and daunting. We had to create a news department and find a sports team, music presenters, and experts in specialist fields, such as health, business, and local and national government.

The way my staff pulled together during this challenging and stressful pre-start up period was incredible. I knew at the time that it was the beginning of great things to come. The magic ingredient was the camaraderie; we were a team, and we were all very proud of our very special radio station.

Several months before we were to air, I was notified by the IBA that the transmitter and masts would be ready for the planned air date of 1 April 1974. I was unhappy with this, not only was it April Fool's Day, which seemed ominous, but also it was a Monday, which meant the staff would have had two days off from practicing the co-ordinated teamwork which needed to be sharp for launch day to run smoothly. I asked the IBA to change the air date to the next day, Tuesday 2 April 1974, and they agreed. This meant every member of staff could be present on the Monday to work out any last-minute problems which might arise.

Leading up to the air date, the IBA played soothing classical music on what was to become Piccadilly Radio's 261m wavelength. This enabled me to check the quality of the signal physically, which was excellent throughout Greater Manchester and well beyond the perimeter of our coverage area.

Finally, the big day arrived. Well before sunrise, our entire team was at the station, along with several directors, a handful of advertisers, and a few friends. There was a nervous tension in the air as everyone prepared for the opening moments of what was to become the country's most successful full service commercial radio station, Piccadilly Radio.

I took a deep breath and waited. A new style of radio was about to hit Manchester's airwaves. At exactly 5am on 2 April 1974, Roger Day greeted the audience for the first time and said these words:

GOOD MORNING, MANCHESTER. THIS IS THE
EXCITING NEW SOUND OF PICCADILLY RADIO.

And the rest, as they say, is radio history …

Philip T. Birch

(Sadly, Philip Birch died on December 7th, 2021, aged ninety-four, just two weeks after writing this foreword.)

Contents

Prologue

Start of a New Era

*I do not think that the radio waves I have
discovered will have any practical application
— Heinrich Hertz (1888)*

2 April 2024 will mark the fiftieth anniversary of Piccadilly Radio's launch to an unsuspecting public across Greater Manchester. In 1974, it was the fifth commercial radio station to hit the airwaves and in a very short time, became the most popular and successful mixed news and entertainment radio station in the country, listened to and loved by millions of people.

In a region which was home to ground-breaking media such as the *Manchester Guardian, Granada Television,* and the *Manchester Evening News,* perhaps it wasn't so surprising that the new radio station would blaze a trail and herald a new dawn in local broadcasting. Its iconic 261 logo and jingles quickly became part of the fabric of everyday life in the Northwest of England.

It was the radio station which spawned the careers of national personalities such as Chris Evans, Timmy Mallett, Gary Davies, Mark Radcliffe, Andy Crane, Steve Penk and Andy Peebles, plus a host of journalists, TV and film producers, businessmen and women and entrepreneurs.

At the same time, it nurtured hugely popular local personalities including Susie Mathis, Phil Wood, Dave Ward, Mike Shaft, James Stannage, Mike Sweeney, Becky Want and Stu Allen, none of whom had ever broadcast before being given the opportunity to join the station. They became part of listeners' daily lives.

The station was launched at a time when the country was in a dire economic situation. The Heath Government had taken on the miners, who were on strike, and planned a three-day working week. Television hours were restricted to save energy and there was a shortage of newsprint. During these huge setbacks, paraffin heaters were used at what was to become the home of Piccadilly Radio when there was no electricity. Offices and studios were not fully constructed, and broadcast desks only arrived two weeks before 'D' Day, leaving little time for rehearsal. They were worrying times for the launch of a business which relied solely on advertising.

The two London stations, Capital and LBC, which had launched in the previous autumn, were experiencing very difficult financial challenges. Yet these setbacks seemed to inspire a team spirit and determination to succeed at Piccadilly, traits which would be the backbone of the organisation throughout its lifespan.

The studios were situated in Piccadilly Plaza overlooking Piccadilly Gardens. On the outside of the building were huge blow-ups of the DJs – big, brash and totally dominating the city centre. Interestingly, the station was built on the site of a former lunatic asylum, which in hindsight seems a totally appropriate location for what would become a pioneering, fearless and, at times, outrageous radio station.

So why was it so successful? Was it luck? A case of the right people at the right time, from DJs to producers, from the sales and promotions teams to the engineers, from the newsroom to reception? Or the fact that it broadcast to the most responsive and the very best of audiences?

The Piccadilly Radio story starts with the 'two Bs' who made it all happen: Anthony Blond and Philip Birch.

Chapter 1

Radio Waves

*The day has come. Tonight, pirate radio dies. From midnight,
we are a ghost ship floating without hope on cold and
dark waters. You have done almighty work here.
Thank you. But your work is done
— Quentin, 'The Boat That Rocked'*

As Philip Radcliffe explains in his excellent book written in 1980, *The Piccadilly Story*, Piccadilly Radio didn't just happen, it was brought about by the vision, enterprise, and determination of many people.

Behind its success lies a fascinating story of radio pirates and party politics, of ambition and achievement. It is set against the background of a revolution in British broadcasting, which saw the BBC's monopoly of public radio stretching back over half a century challenged.

The first threat came in the 1960s from the so-called 'pirates' who started beaming a new kind of popular commercial broadcasting to British listeners from ships three miles off the coast, thereby uncovering a vast audience with an appetite for a kind of programme not provided by the BBC. The most popular pirate stations, by far, were Radio Caroline and Radio London.

The inevitable emergence of Independent Local Radio in the next decade repulsed that challenge, as new laws of the land were passed, none more significant than the Government's Marine Offences 1967 Act. This piece of legislation put the pirates out of business and forced the BBC to acknowledge that there was a demand for popular music programming.

In 1967, the BBC changed from broadcasting the 'Third', 'Home' and 'Light' programmes to the newly-named Radios 1,

2, 3 and 4. Also, in 1970, it started to introduce its local radio stations in an effort to silence its critics and pre-empt any move towards local commercial radio.

Ironically, it legitimised many of the pirate DJs by signing the likes of Radio London's Tony Blackburn, Kenny Everett and Dave Cash to Radio 1. When the Conservative Party won the 1970 General Election, they too were committed to local radio, but paid for by advertising, not the public. It did not take them long to publish a White Paper, 'An Alternative Service of Local Broadcasting'.

Despite opposition from the Labour Party, the Government pushed on and in 1972 announced the locations of a projected twenty-six Independent Local Radio (ILR) stations and the newly formed Independent Broadcasting Authority (IBA). The IBA initially invited applications for the first five stations, two in London as well as Glasgow, Birmingham and Manchester.

To sort out the serious contenders from the pipe-dreamers, the Authority spelt out the detailed programme plans and financial arrangements required. As far as Manchester was concerned, it provided a footprint of the area to be covered and allocated the frequencies: 261 Medium Wave and 97.0 VHF. It also stated what the rental initially payable to the Authority for the contract would be: £108,000 in year one, £120,000 in year two and £132,000 in year three (the equivalent of £1.3 million in 2022!).

The Authority also made provision for a 'secondary rental', which in effect meant that if the station made a profit over a certain amount, it would have to pay a proportion back to the Authority to be ploughed back into improvements and renewals of technical equipment.

The critics of the time argued that commercial radio stations would be 'all pop and prattle and a licence to print money'. The reality was that the new stations had to stick to rigorous programming requirements and pay the Radio

Authority for the right to be, while competing against the BBC national and local radio stations … which were funded from the public purse!

The race to win the chance to run the new commercial radio station in Manchester began. Various groups and individuals started organising themselves into syndicates to bid for the franchise. The early front runners included Manchester's Radio Voice Ltd., considered to be unbeatable. It was led by Lord Hewlett, a Tory politician and well-known Mancunian, and included the *Guardian, Manchester Evening News* and Rediffusion, a very strong combination of local knowledge and technical expertise. They were widely considered to be the favourites for the licence. The other group, Red Rose Radio Ltd., was headed by disc jockey, Brian Mathews and included world famous astronomer, Professor Sir Bernard Lovell and DJ, Jimmy Savile.

The third, which was initially considered the rank outsider, brought together two men who together made the dream a reality. One, the maverick Anthony Blond, was responsible for laying the foundations of Piccadilly Radio; the other, Philip Birch, for setting Piccadilly Radio up and running it. As Philip Radcliffe commented in his book, 'They couldn't have been more dissimilar, but the one quality they shared was entrepreneurship - one inspired the other'.

Anthony Blond was an extrovert character and publisher who regularly appeared in the national newspaper gossip columns under the heading, 'Blonds have more fun'. His Wikipedia page explains that he was born in Sale, educated at Eton and served his National Service in the army (but registered as a conscientious objector). Having gained a history scholarship to New College Oxford, he lost it, having been distracted by undergraduate life, or as he described it, 'the joys of drink, people, parties, fancy waistcoats, foreign travel and falling in love - mostly with young men'. He was an ebullient showman of the highest order.

The maverick Anthony Blond, the person responsible
for laying the foundations of Piccadilly Radio.

Philip Birch, meanwhile, although born in Winnipeg, was
from a middle-class family in Kent, a grammar school boy who
became an army infantry officer in his teens. Seeking his fortune,
he moved to America and in the late 1950s, was one of the
original 'Mad Men', an advertising executive working for J.
Walter Thompson on Madison Avenue in New York. A softly
spoken, urbane, erudite, imposing figure, he was the opposite of
Anthony Blond, but they became a very formidable team.

When one of Philip's clients, who owned a Ford
dealership in Texas, heard about the pirate radio stations in
England, he suggested they got in on the act. Philip resigned

from JWT after fifteen years' service, raised half a million pounds, mainly from American backers, bought a ship with a Dutch crew and launched Radio London. Simple. During the three years it existed, 'Big L' became by far the most successful pirate station of them all, making a profit of over three million pounds.

Blond, meanwhile, frustrated by not being able to get involved in the two London franchises, turned his attention to Manchester and set about bringing a consortium together. He was tenacious. Over drinks, lunches, dinners and telephone calls, he drew in an unlikely range of potential investors. Norman Quick, the Manchester car dealer; Granada Television; St. Regis newspapers, who published the *Bolton Evening News* and the Lancashire Journal Series; and local newspaper groups from Rochdale, Bury, Warrington, St. Helens, Ashton-under-Lyne, and Stockport. The group would also eventually include the Co-operative Wholesale Society in Bolton, Wigan, and Oldham.

Blond was an extraordinary and persuasive character. At their first ever meeting, Norman Quick wrote him a personal cheque for five hundred pounds (over six thousand pounds in today's money) to 'get on with it'. Later, he would recall that Sidney Friedland, managing director of Northern Commercial Trust, sat on the edge of his bed in the Midland Hotel and promised to lend him one hundred and sixty thousand pounds (almost two million pounds today) after he failed to arouse any interest from friends in the City. Friedland would continue to back him all the way.

Special mention must be made here for Joe Wilmott, managing director of St. Regis Newspapers, who Blond described as 'my first and loyal ally'. He fought hard to convince his less than enthusiastic board of directors to invest in this new venture and provided seed capital to maintain momentum. Wilmott would go on to be the second chairman of the company.

By 1972, Blond's 'dark horse' syndicate was coming up fast on its rivals. Greater Manchester Independent Radio (GMIR) was becoming a serious player. (As he mentioned in his Foreword, Philip Birch would point out that GMIR was an anagram of GRIM ... his choice of Piccadilly Radio for the station soon changed that!) Having secured the necessary funding from shareholders (interestingly, a one-pound share would be worth ten times that four years later) the next hurdle was to put together the formal written application to the IBA.

Chapter 2

The Application

The River Irwell has a better claim than the Nile, Indus, Tigris or Euphrates, to be the epicentre of current world civilisation
— Philip Radcliffe, 'The Piccadilly Story'

It was 1973.

OPEC announced the restriction of the flow of oil, causing the price of oil to increase by two hundred per cent.

Britain and Ireland joined the European Economic Community.

The World Trade Centre became the tallest building in the world.

LBC became the first legal commercial radio station.

Ryan Giggs was born. In a twenty-four-year career, he would play over six hundred and fifty games for Manchester United scoring one hundred and fourteen goals.

At the Oscars, *The Godfather* won the award for Best Picture

In a major upset, second division Sunderland beat the mighty Leeds United in the FA Cup Final.

Last of the Summer Wine began its first series. There would be thirty that followed with the last episode of the thirty-first series being filmed in 2010.

Carly Simon's *You're So Vain* was released.

And Piccadilly Radio's consortium applied for the Manchester franchise.

***

The quote above about the River Irwell, noted by Philip Radcliffe in *The Piccadilly Story*, as he continued to point out, 'was but one of many bold - and absurd - statements in Greater Manchester Independent Radio's application to the IBA for the Manchester commercial radio franchise. Likewise, for some of the early programme ideas. *Coronation Street* and *Crown Court* without the pictures. Fan clubs for Verdi and Louis Armstrong. A Poet Laureate in residence. Dramas and musicals about building railways in the Northwest. Tips on training whippets. Advice on how to cope with a husband who doesn't love you anymore'.

The written submission had Anthony Blond's hand all over it. Funny, outrageous, thought provoking and fiercely 'Northern'. The opening paragraph alone set the tone, not only for the rest of the document, but also for the ethos and values of the future radio station. Yet, it's that imaginative thinking that gave the document a refreshing readability and appeal. The submission threw in a plethora of ludicrous programming ideas but, as we will read later, those ideas weren't that far off the mark.

Meanwhile, the submission wasn't slow at coming forward and having a pop at the BBC's local radio station, either while complimenting its 'high minded competence' or asserting that it had 'failed to excite the audience or command their allegiance'. (In the years that followed, Piccadilly's independent audience research would show that at times, the station had seven times as many listeners as its BBC counterpart.)

The submission's approach to news was to present and interpret the national news agenda's relevance to Greater Manchester. 'If there's a national dock dispute, then the impact on Manchester docks will be considered. If there's a fall in the national unemployment figures, but a marginal increase in Lancashire figures, the latter will be examined. A new Act of Parliament will be explained only for its impact on the Manchester area'. And more; 'That is not parochialism, it is a common-sense service to a community which is frequently ill served by the metropolitan thinking of national news organisations.' The message, quite simply, was 'Up yours London'.

On a more personal level, the consortium promised to provide a Citizens' Advice and Action Service to offer support on a whole range of problems: personal, domestic, consumer, medical, legal, social security etc. Too ambitious for its time? Not so, the Piccadilly Family Care Line, an independent advice service, was set up and funded by the station in 1979 and helped thousands of Northwest people with helpful, practical, and confidential advice. A little more, then, than 'pop and prattle'.

Bursting with ideas, promises and idealism, the document was backed up with a market research survey which showed, amongst other things, that 'there was no concept of Greater Manchester' and that there was 'little confidence or interest in local radio, largely due to the weak identity of Radio Manchester'. A broader regional identity existed, and respondents wanted a station that was 'active, campaigning, helpful, informative, friendly, relaxed and somewhat youthful'.

The document was submitted to the IBA in December 1972.

As Philip Radcliffe again notes in his book, *The Piccadilly Story*, 'despite all the planning, the GMIR team was by no means match fit for the semi-final, an on-the-spot IBA selection interview on 11 January 1973 at the Midland Hotel in Manchester. The captain, Neil Pearson, a highly respected lawyer who had agreed to be the founding chairman, was away in Ethiopia of all places and some members of the team had not even met each other, let alone played together. "Some of us met for the first time getting out of the lift to go to the meeting!" said one director. "It was pretty disorganised."'

Despite the shortcomings, the motley crew impressed the IBA deputation sufficiently enough to be selected for the final interview, fixed for March in London. Manchester's Radio Voice group also survived, but the Red Rose Group, which promised 'entertainment all the way', was eliminated. Having overcome the first hurdle, Blond recognised that they had a lot of work to do before the final presentation.

The consortium acknowledged that the absence of a chief executive was a major weakness. Time was running out, but then cometh the hour, cometh the man … Philip Birch. The former pirate was currently working for Associated Newspapers, directing their bid for London's all-news station, but the franchise had gone to LBC. He was the outstanding candidate and more importantly, he was available. In retrospect, it appears that the IBA may have encouraged Birch to join GMIR and suggested to the consortium that he could be the missing piece of the jigsaw.

So, at last, the 'two Bs' came together. Blond, the ultimate showman and non-stop networker and Birch, the astute businessman who understood radio better than anyone at the time. Philip fronted the final interview and on 5 March 1973 Chairman, Neil Pearson, rang Norman Quick and uttered the fateful words, "Our lot's got it!"

Chapter 3

A Leader Who Created Leaders

*This was a radio station where everything was groovier than
anything that had been groovy before. Piccadilly Radio
knew exactly who it was and what it was about.
It was a new voice for a new generation. It was about
the Northwest and everyone who lived there
— Chris Evans, 'It's Not What You Think'*

It was 1974.

A 'Three Day Week' was introduced on 1 January.

The women of *Coronation Street* won a holiday in the Bahamas which they swapped for a holiday in Majorca.

Richard Nixon became the first American President to resign.

On the last full day of the 1973-74 season, Manchester United were relegated from Division 1. Former United player Denis Law, playing for Manchester City, scored a goal against his old team but didn't celebrate.

West Germany won the 1974 World Cup at home in Munich … and not on penalties.

Mud had the year's best-selling single with *Tiger Feet*.

Blazing Saddles was the big box office hit.

Jaws by Peter Benchley was one of the year's best-selling books.

And Piccadilly Radio was launched, with those first iconic jingles commissioned from CCS (Collective Consciousness Society) a group of mainly studio musicians, who as the band C.C.S. recorded the instrumental version of *Whole Lotta Love*, the theme for *Top of the Pops*.

***

It's one thing to propose a programming philosophy in a written submission, but quite another to create a schedule which reflects its broad intentions and at the same time, appeals to a brand-new audience. To achieve this, Philip Birch had to appoint the most important member of staff, the programme controller, the person who would be responsible for the entire output of the new station. That person was Colin Walters and his contribution to the success of Piccadilly Radio was immense.

At just twenty-eight years of age, Walters had become the BBC's youngest station manager at Radio Nottingham. He had joined the station four years earlier as a journalist and had quickly risen through the ranks. In Autumn 1973, he sent a somewhat threatening memo to all Radio Nottingham contract staff:

> You will be aware that commercial radio is in the process of recruiting in London, Birmingham and Manchester for stations that are about to open. I just want all Radio Nottingham staff to know that anyone who is discovered to be in negotiations with independent radio stations will have their contract terminated immediately.

The enigmatic Walters then not only joined Piccadilly Radio in January 1974, but later poached Radio Nottingham's Roger Finnegan and Stephen Beard to head up the station's features department!

Aged just thirty-one and standing at six feet four inches, he was an imposing figure, arrogant, direct, articulate and someone who regularly conducted job interviews with his feet on his desk. He was never afraid to hand out proper bollockings - in public - often using choice language. At the same time, he was a daring, imaginative, forward thinking radio man through and through. He was the radio equivalent of Alex Ferguson, capable of the hairdryer treatment one minute, but then he would put his arm around you the next and in most cases defend you against any criticism. He was much loved and respected by his team and many of the people who worked for him went on to bigger things, because Walters inspired them to believe that they could.

The larger-than-life Colin Walters

The task of recruiting over forty members of programming staff in less than four months was daunting. Presenters, journalists, sports reporters, features editors, technical operators, and broadcast assistants, all had to be interviewed and appointed and not all of them had broadcasting experience. Add to this the fact that the studios were nowhere near complete, equipment was delayed and staff had to use second hand desks and chairs that Granada TV had donated, it's perhaps little wonder that Walters could appear extremely grumpy at times.

As the early audience research had shown, people had no concept of 'Greater Manchester', (in fact, Greater Manchester only became a designated functional City Region on 1 April 1974 … the day before the station went on air). One of the reasons that BBC Radio Manchester's audience figures were less than impressive was that folk in Bolton, Wigan, Oldham and the other boroughs didn't associate with Manchester. They all had - and still have - their own identity, accents … and climates!

Despite not being from the region, Walters quickly sensed the mood of the moment and in a stroke of genius, the station didn't talk about being in 'Greater Manchester'. It was 'Piccadilly Land … Piccadilly News … Piccadilly Weather … Piccadilly Sport'. There were no 'Golden Oldies', it was 'Piccadilly Magic'. The station owned it all. Walters knew what listeners in the ten boroughs would relate to.

But where were the new station's DJs going to come from? Most of the ex-pirates had been snapped up by Radios 1 and 2. Capital Radio in London had launched six months earlier with some excellent presenters and BBC local radio wasn't producing the type of personnel Colin was looking for.

The United Biscuit Network (UBN) was one source for presenters who were at least experienced in pop music formats. UBN was an in-house radio station which entertained workers in United Biscuits' factories across the country, literally playing requests for 'all the girls and guys on the chocolate digestive production line this morning.' Roger Day (who is still broadcasting), Pete Reeves (who in his later career would write cartoon scripts for *Pingu* and *Postman Pat*) and Steve Merrick, were recruited by Walters from UBN. Other presenters came from various backgrounds, most with no broadcast experience, but people who Walters thought had potential. Indeed, 'Appoint on potential' was one of his maxims.

In many ways, in the early days, the station was structured along the lines of BBC local radio. In some respects, it was pitched somewhere between Radios 1 and 4, popular music daytime shows, but with a mid-day features programme, *Piccadilly Central* and a heavy emphasis on half hour lunchtime and early evening news bulletins. Phone-ins were an important part of a day's output, as were outside broadcasts from factories and shopping centres.

Sport was part of the station's DNA, with the team led by Tom Tyrell covering all the football, cricket and rugby league news and fixtures. Weekday early evenings would include folk with Harry Ogden; country and western with Joe Fish; and rock shows with Chris Tetley, with coverage of mid-week football matches seamlessly merged into the programmes. Despite this somewhat predictable format, the new station was a breath of fresh air to listeners across the Northwest. It played requests from people who lived in your local area, covered local events and was highly visible, with outside broadcasts and events. You felt it belonged to you and that you were a part of it.

And at the heart of Piccadilly Radio was the unique individual that was Colin Walters. One Friday afternoon, the co-authors of this book were given the address of a building in Swinton by Walters and instructed to be there at ten o'clock the next morning, without being told why. You didn't argue with Walters so, dutifully, we arrived on time the next morning to discover that together with his son, Joe, we were witnesses to his wedding to journalist, Petrina Rance. No lavish wedding breakfast, just bacon butties at their house, after which he took his new wife to Maine Road to watch Manchester City. Radio's Mr. Darcy didn't stop the romance there, either. The next day, the newly married couple went to Flamborough Head. Petrina stayed in the hotel, while Walters went birdwatching. And for one weekend only, the green light in the on-air studio – Walters' personal line to the presenter – didn't flash for forty-eight hours …

Roger Day, the former pirate disc jockey, who said the famous first words, "Good morning, Manchester – This is the exiting new sound of Piccadilly Radio," on 2 April 1974.

Piccadilly Radio was launched officially at 5am on Tuesday 2 April 1974, the decision being taken not to launch on 1 April for obvious reasons, as noted. It was decided, as mentioned previously by Philip Birch, not to call it Greater Manchester Independent Radio, its official name, as the possibility of it being rearranged into GRIM was felt, not surprisingly, to be inappropriate. Launch day in the middle of the three-day week was organised chaos, which could perhaps have been anticipated because, as previously mentioned, the radio station had been built on the site of the former Manchester Lunatic Asylum, which had stood there from 1756 for a grim eighty-five years.

Studio equipment arrived with only a couple of weeks to go, leaving little time for rehearsal. As Roger Day, the former pirate disc jockey, said the famous first words, "Good morning, Manchester – This is the exciting new sound of Piccadilly Radio," the Beach Boys' *Good Vibrations* wowed in as he hadn't cued the record up properly. The first news bulletin lasted seven and a half minutes, instead of the scheduled five, and the news reader dried … but recovered. Despite its dodgy start, Piccadilly Radio was up and running and was destined to become one of the UK's most successful radio stations ever.

***

I was there at the start. I was getting ready to begin my first year in secondary school. I remember hearing the opening notes of 'Good Vibrations' and being welcomed to ILR Manchester.

Piccadilly Radio became my companion throughout my teenage years, Stannage, Phil Wood, Jim Reeve and the other presenters were always part of my listening landscape.

Piccadilly Radio is part of my DNA and I'm so glad I was lucky enough to be around when it was at its best.

John Brookes, Dallas, Texas

***

Don't touch that dial …

Chapter 4

Reception: A Window to the World

On the inside of Piccadilly Radio's reception was a flashing map, like a pin ball machine, demonstrating dramatically that Piccadilly Radio was not just of a city, but of a whole region
— Philip Radcliffe, 'The Piccadilly Story'

It was 1975.

The Vietnam War ended, with Communist forces seizing control of South Vietnam. The country was unified as the Socialist Republic of Vietnam the following year.

Gary Neville, Nicky Butt and David Beckham were born.

Manchester United clinched promotion to the First Division, one season after being relegated.

Two new laws, the Sex Discrimination Act 1975 and the Equal Pay Act 1970, came into force aiming to end unequal pay of men and women in the workplace.

Margaret Thatcher defeated Edward Heath in the Conservative Party leadership election, becoming the party's first female leader.

Monty Python and The Holy Grail was released.

The first episode of *Fawlty Towers* was broadcast on BBC2.

Queen's *Bohemian Rhapsody* was released.

The Sex Pistols made their first public performance.

It snowed in June.

And at Piccadilly Radio, Martha Burgess taught Eric Morecambe how to use the switch board. He sat with her on reception for over half an hour answering calls!

***

Piccadilly Radio was based in an architectural disaster known as Piccadilly Plaza, under a tower block hotel and above the Olde English Chippie and Brentford Nylons. People often wandered up to the open piazza on the first floor by mistake and could find themselves entombed there for hours, wandering around the concrete jungle.

Piccadilly Radio studios dominated the city centre.
'Where the music and the magic was found in equal measure'.

In his brilliant book, *Thank You for the Days*, Mark Radcliffe remembers his place of work with 'affection' – 'There was even a crazy golf course up there at one point and, also, a duck pond. Unfortunately, on the day of the grand opening, the specially installed ducks had taken one look at their proposed new habitat and flown off through the open skylights into the wide blue yonder. The forlorn deserted pond was then drained of all liquids save the odd pool of tramps' urine and served as a large rubbish bin thereafter'.

Piccadilly Radio's receptionists were almost as famous as its presenters. Philip Radcliffe, Mark's father, paints the perfect picture of them '… girls elevated like high priestesses welcome a stream of casual callers'. People asking for stickers, a signed photograph of their favourite presenter, a record request for Auntie Betty; to drop off an egg for the Easter Egg Appeal or something for the Christmas Toy and Tin Appeal; or to catch a glimpse of their favourite pop star who they knew was going to be on air that day.

The legendary Pat Broome was the highest of the high priestesses. Nothing and no one got past her. She was ably assisted by a bevy of other receptionists - Martha, Deborah, Karen, Michelle, and Eve (who was more entertaining than any of the presenters!). One night, Eve walked into the newsroom with a post card in her hand, asking, "What's a noddy holder?" Only Eve could have confused the lead singer of Slade with a pouch to hold condoms.

And there's more. Eve spilling a can of Special Brew into the switchboard, thus putting the 999 service out of action. Eve putting a pie in the new-fangled microwave and setting it to cook for twenty-five minutes, which prompted a visit from the fire brigade. And when Eve had her hours reduced to one Monday a week, she submitted a holiday form. As she was entitled to twenty-eight days' holiday, she wanted to book twenty-eight Mondays, meaning she'd have more than half the year off.

One extraordinary thing about the early years of Piccadilly Radio was the high quality of the live guests who came through the doors. These were not simply music guests, which you'd expect from a music-based station. They were, of course, there -

Debbie Harry, Marc Bolan, Kate Bush, Cliff Richard, Bryan Ferry etc. There were others, though, because the technology and available media of the day dictated that the biggest names had to make the journey north.

There were 'A' list film stars and stage actors - Sophia Loren, Anthony Hopkins, Derek Jacobi, Joan Collins, Omar Sharif. Politicians such as Margaret Thatcher and naturalists and adventurers such as David Attenborough all did major live interviews for Piccadilly and these appearances were not rarities. The Plaza was often full of listeners waiting to catch a glimpse of their favourite pop star, film star or politician. Okay, two out of three ain't bad …

They say that you should never meet your heroes, but they were different times and celebrities were somewhat more approachable than today's wannabes.

Jayne Mansell was one of the hardworking technical staff and recalls the day that she shared a brew with a singing sensation:

> When guests came in for interview, they were normally taken from reception to be seated on the comfy couch outside Master Control Room and normally had an entourage with them. Just after Annie Lennox went solo and was clocking up the hits, she was booked for interview on an evening show. I was on duty and standing in reception waiting for her party to arrive.
>
> A lady came wandering down the piazza towards reception. It was Annie Lennox on her own. Strange, I thought. I greeted her and the first thing she asked was my name, how I was and what did I do, but in a way of true interest. We chatted like old friends as I walked her through to the couch outside the studio.
>
> I explained I would take her through to the studio and asked if she would like a drink, advising against the machine stuff. Instead, I would go to the kitchen and make a proper brew. She asked where the kitchen was; I sort of pointed in the general

direction. She stood up and asked what I drank and insisted on making me a brew, which she did. A genuinely nice person.

George Best was a regular visitor to the station and at one point, after he'd stopped playing, he did several *Saturday Sports* phone-ins ... and never missed a show. He was paid five hundred pounds a programme, but just before going on air, his then manager came in with a bag full of dodgy Gucci watches which were offered to staff at a 'very good price'. Like we said, never meet your heroes ...

Spike Milligan was once found standing on the sofa in reception, trying to remove the loudspeaker in the ceiling.

"Can I help you?" he was asked.

"No," he said. "I'm just trying to disable the muzak."

Many of the guests stayed at the Piccadilly Hotel when they were in town, and it wasn't unusual for them to listen to Piccadilly Radio late into the night in their hotel bedroom. Freddie Starr phoned in and asked if he could come and sit in on the *Night Beat* show, which he did until the early hours of the morning.

Graham Nash phoned once after the presenter, Roger Day, had played a Hollies track and asked Roger why he didn't play one with him on. As a result, Nash came in for a memorable guest spot and played *Just A Song Before You Go,* on the piano, which he had just written. The BBC were particularly peeved as they had been trying to get him on for years.

Producer Hazel Murray remembers her own late celebrity encounter:

> For a while, the daytime producers took turns to be overnight producers to try and increase the listening figures. One night when I was on, we were expecting Demis Roussos in. He did eventually manage to get to the studio, but first came the famous incident of the guard on the roof saying something like, "Denis who? I don't care who you are mate, you can't park there."

A massive star at the time, Warren Beatty, was directing the 1981 film *Reds* at the Zion Centre on Stratford Road in Hulme, which doubled as Chicago Town Hall. He couldn't make it to the studio because of his hectic schedule, but agreed to be interviewed by Tim Grundy during a break in filming. The station extensively trailed the 'Hollywood star exclusive interview'.

When Tim returned to the studio, he realised there was a problem with the tape and the interview was unusable. Tim went back to where Beatty was filming and waited and waited. Around 11pm, Beatty was leaving the set and he spotted Tim.

"What are you still doing here?" he asked.

Tim explained the problem.

Beatty took a breath, paused, looked Tim in the eye and said, "Well, we'd better do it again then."

Class.

Henry Matthews was one of the best known of the Piccadilly news readers. It is, though, his very first day on the job that he remembers most vividly as it was, in his words, "the day I lost my virginity."

I had been taken somewhat by surprise when, as a freelance, I was summoned to do a news reading shift. Having diligently prepared the bulletin for the top of the hour, I asked the then news editor, Mike Hill, what I should do with it. To my surprise, I was told, "Well go in the studio and read it of course!" And so, petrified, I went in and read it. Not what I had expected at all, but that was to prove the least of my worries.

I grew in confidence with every bulletin. Five minutes on top of the hour, and thirty seconds of headlines on the half hour and by the time my shift drew to a close, it had become a bit of a breeze! At mid-day, I read the news into a programme called *Piccadilly Central*, a rather good topical talk show presented by Roger Finnegan and Phil Griffin.

That morning, they had a rather special guest. I was a fan of his and in my teens, I never missed a show. I never expected to meet him quite in the way I did. Reading the half-hour headlines, I heard the studio door opening quietly behind me. I expected to be handed a piece of paper informing me of, what they call these days, 'Breaking News'. But nothing materialised and of course, I couldn't turn away from the mic to find out what was going on.

I then realised I had been joined in the studio by a chicken. All I could hear were chicken noises. I ploughed on regardless and by the time the longest thirty seconds in my life had elapsed, I turned to look for the chicken. It had already disappeared. I was loathe to mention it back in the newsroom for fear of creating the impression that it all been too much for me and I'd flipped. I had only got one bulletin to go - the one o'clock - and could then disappear for a large brandy.

But it wasn't quite over yet. Lightning, it seems, was going to strike twice. Halfway through the bulletin, once again I heard the studio door opening behind me and immediately thought, 'It's that bloody chicken again!' Again, I ploughed on expecting any moment to hear clucking noises. The climax of the chicken's performance came during a very heavy story about the IRA bombing campaign in Northern Ireland. As I put on my most solemn voice to recount an incident of shooting or other carnage, 'the chicken' cupped his hands to his mouth and shouted in a classic Goons voice, "It's all lies folks!" That large brandy became an ever-greater necessity although by now, of course, I realised my chicken and unexpected intruder who had taken it upon himself to join me was the guest from Roger and Phil's show … Spike Milligan.

Now, someone took it upon themselves to inform Spike that it was, in fact, my very first day behind a microphone. He was mortified. He came into the newsroom where he offered a fulsome apology. Nonchalantly, I replied, "Think nothing of it," but suspect the sweat on my brow was a bit of a giveaway!

Spike was doing a one-man show at the Palace Theatre and to make amends, invited me along that night as his guest, telling me I could also take along my wife, my girlfriend, my boyfriend or all three if I chose and we would then all join him for dinner at the Midland Hotel. Now, I was pencilled in for the same early shift the following day … and decided I needed an early night, so I declined. I've regretted it ever since!

When guests came in to plug a book, it was accepted by the publicist accompanying the author that he or she would sign the book and put a pithy personal message underneath it. Producer Simon Cole naively thought that Jeffrey Archer meant it when he signed a copy of his book with a line saying it was the best interview he'd done … only to discover when talking to Alex Dickson at Radio Clyde some years later, that Archer wrote that in everyone's copy.

Tony Ingham's first brush with celebrities came during the three-day week, six weeks before launch:

I asked the Carpenters' record company to hold their press conference in the studios of the UK's newest commercial radio station. The record company agreed; the media gathered; and the pair arrived with their manager. One slight problem was that the studio equipment hadn't arrived, so all there was to see were empty rooms, with a few builders knocking about.

Valiantly, I started to explain the studio layout, but it was getting embarrassing, so quickly thinking on my feet, I asked if they would grab a couple of saws and pretend that they were helping to build the studios. The Carpenters building … get it?

Their manager, Sherwin Bash, says, "We're not doing that Tony."

I say, "Come on, give me a break here." (Media with cameras at the ready, remember.)

"Nope," was the reply.

"Why not?" I asked.

"Because if they were called the Plumbers, would you expect them to crawl down fucking pipes ?!?" and they just walked out and left me standing there with a chisel in my hands.

And sound engineer, Pete Johnson, remembers December 1984 for a very special reason:

We were recording Bob Geldof and the Boomtown Rats at the Apollo. The afternoon rehearsal over, Bob Geldof came into our truck to hear what we had, then started to talk with the producer, Simon Cole, about an idea he'd had for a large fund-raising concert with masses of big names. Did we think commercial radio and Piccadilly would be interested? A few months later and it's the summer of 1985 and Live Aid ...

For some reason, any unusual calls to the switchboard on reception were put through to the promotions manager. On one occasion, the caller wanted more than a signed photograph of Dave Ward, as Tony Ingham recalls:

On the day before Good Friday, around lunchtime, Pat on reception called to tell me that there was a man on the phone who wanted to speak to someone in charge. If not, he said that there would be big trouble. I took the call. He told me that there was a bomb in the radio station, that he wanted five thousand pounds in cash, or he'd, "Blow the fucking place up." He said that I had just thirty minutes to sort it.

We got lots of crank calls, so I knew the procedure: Call the police and do a search. The big problem, though, was that we'd had our annual Easter Egg collection for children in the Northwest, who otherwise wouldn't have got anything. Lots had already been sent out, but there were still hundreds in reception.

Within minutes, CID turned up. They bugged my phone to a speaker, and we chatted away, waiting for the caller to phone back, which – apparently - they didn't, usually. He did. This was unusual. He asked if I'd got the money and the police nodded at me to say that I had. I'm told by the caller to put the money in a large brown envelope with a Piccadilly Radio sticker on it, to leave the building, walk down Market Street along Cross Street, enter Victoria Station and wait under the clock. I'm warned that if I called the police, Piccadilly Radio would be blown up. No pressure, then.

For some reason I still don't understand. I'm volunteered to take an envelope stuffed with a copy of the MEN *(Manchester Evening News)* and told to do as he says, but not to worry as there would be police watching my every move. I walked the walk and stood under the clock at Victoria Station. After fifteen minutes, a plain clothes policeman walked past me eating an apple and whispered, "Go back to the station."

Back in the office and we all enjoy a cup of tea. Pat comes through. "It's him again," she tells me.

Him. "You fucking bastard, you told the police, you've sealed off the entrance to your building."

Me. "No. I've told security, we can't have the public coming in. It's normal practice if we have a threat and listen, if you have put a bomb in an Easter egg most of them have already gone out."

Him. "You've got twenty minutes to get back there. If I get caught, my mate will fucking blow it."

'Yea right', I think. Then I looked at the two police officers who had gone white.

"They never call back," they'd said. "You have to go and meet him," they insist.

"Whoa, me?" I ask.

"Yes, he's already seen you," they confirm.
Next minute, I was in a black cab with an armed police officer on the floor and told to keep calm.

They continued, "But … if he approaches, he must get a hand on the envelope and take it from you. Don't worry, there's lots of police cover there."

I'm back under the clock, smoking, when a pair of hobnail boots approached, and someone asked for a light.

"'Is this for you?" I asked.

"What?" he replied.

"Er nothing, sorry," I confirmed.

He looked round and said, "Is the money in there?"(It wasn't, it just still had the day's copy of the MEN it in!)

"Yes," I say, "but listen, if there is a bomb, almost all the Easter eggs have gone out."

Pause. "Follow me," he says. My legs have now turned to jelly.

"No way, I'm going nowhere."

He grabbed the envelope, and all hell broke loose. A policeman dived over my shoulder … and failed to grab him. He set off up the platform, pursued by several other policemen. I got pinned to the floor and handcuffed, despite telling them I'm the good guy. As I'm frog marched along the platform, I was greeted by a chap I knew who was delivering magazines to W.H. Smith.

"Hello Tony, everything alright?"

"Yes, I'm fine thanks Chris, bit of a misunderstanding."

I was bustled into a police car and taken to Bootle Street Police Station, before being released. The caller got caught hiding in a signal box further along the line and was sentenced to seven years for demanding money with menaces. Earlier that day, he'd threatened a factory owner in Oldham saying he was holding his family hostage. I'm still not sure that this was in my job spec!

And an urban myth has it that Caroline Aherne developed her Mrs. Merton character with Frank Sidebottom for his show on Piccadilly Radio where she worked as a receptionist. She didn't work there, but Mrs. Merton was a Chris Sievey/Frank Sidebottom creation – Frank's neighbour – and Caroline did play her, then subsequently retained the name for her far more commercially successful version.

Piccadilly Radio reception, welcoming and friendly, staff almost as famous as the presenters. 'Girls elevated like high priestesses' welcomed a stream of casual callers.

Chapter 5

Presenters – The Early Days

*The old idea that all you have to do is put a monkey
in the studio with a pile of records is gone
— Colin Walters, Programme Controller, Piccadilly Radio*

It was 1976.

The worst drought on record hit Britain forcing the use of standpipes.

Irish rock band U2 was formed after drummer Larry Mullen Jr. put a post-it note on the noticeboard of his Dublin school seeking members for a band.

The Apple Computer Company was formed by Steve Jobs and Steve Wozniak.

The first commercial Concorde flights took off.

The Double Decker, Everlasting Gobstopper and Honey Monster Puffs were launched.

The Sex Pistols unleashed several four-letter words on Bill Grundy's early evening TV show. Their Piccadilly Radio interview a week later had to be pre-recorded as a precaution.

Second division Southampton beat first division Manchester United 1-0 in the FA Cup Final with a clearly offside goal from Bobby Stokes in the eighty-third minute.

And Piccadilly Radio welcomed Brotherhood of Man in the week they had won the Eurovision Song Contest with *Save Your Kisses for Me*, as they honoured a long-held booking at Wythenshawe's Golden Garter Club.

***

Even with a steady start, Walters would later admit that, at times, the station was a little too focussed on public service broadcasting. He also recognised that some of his presenters weren't attracting the size of audiences expected, whether it was because they weren't 'Northern' enough and so the listeners didn't relate to them, or simply because Walters just didn't like them. Sadly, Walters passed away in 2019, aged seventy-seven, so we will never know, but he wasn't slow in changing personnel.

There were notable exceptions. Andy Peebles was the in-house DJ at Hardrock in Stretford. His smooth style of presentation, coupled with exceptional music knowledge, had an immediate impact with the Piccadilly audience. His midweek *Rockzac* show attracted major stars such as Elton John and Roger Daltrey to the studio. Record companies were queuing up to get their artistes featured. Andy's Sunday evening *Soul Train* show was so popular that fans from as far away as Leeds would write to say they actually drove into the transmission area to listen to it.

A year after the launch, the *Daily Express* ran a feature saying, 'Here was a local DJ with his finger on the nation's musical pulse'. Warner Brothers record label even produced an *Andy Peebles Soul Train* compilation album, such was his appeal. Through the radio gossip network, it was clear that Radio 1 were keeping an eye on this new kind of music radio presenter. Articulate, credible, with a great voice, and at a time when there was a growing concern within the BBC that Radio 1 was still broadcasting in a style that Harry Enfield would later lampoon with his 'Smashie and Nicey' DJs. It wasn't very surprising then, that following 10cc's Graham Gouldman's claim in a national music paper that Andy was, 'the best radio DJ in the country', Radio 1 came and hired him.

Andy still has very fond memories of his time at Piccadilly, returning in 1984 to present a special edition of *Soul Train*, being one of his favourites.

As he recalls:

My lasting memory, though, is after the show when I was having a meal in the Piccadilly Hotel. The newsreader, John Smithson, came to the table to tell us that Marvin Gaye had been shot dead by his own father.

I left the table and went and recorded a short tribute for one of my favourite singers.

As we will see, Andy Peebles wouldn't be the last acquisition from Piccadilly Radio by the BBC.

A year after the launch of Piccadilly Radio, the *Daily Express* ran a feature saying, 'Andy Peebles, a local DJ with his finger on the nation's musical pulse'.

***

Circa 1975: I was a sixteen-year-old lad. I took the train from Newton-le-Willows and remember going up the tower to get my free window sticker. James Stannage walked in ahead of his show with a Boddingtons six pack. I was an avid listener and got the work radio retuned from some tweedy old station!

Best regards, Steve Perks

***

James Stannage was a former actor and secondary school teacher who joined the fledgling station as a broadcast assistant, so basically, a dogsbody. Following a family visit to America, he returned having listened to a radio 'Shock Jock' and being naturally gobby, suggested to Colin Walters that he should host a late-night phone in, where he could basically be outrageous and insult listeners whose views he disagreed with. There can't have been many programme controllers at that time who would take a gamble like that, but as he would do many times in the future, Walters took it … and it worked.

James Stannage – The nation's first 'shock jock'.

***

James Stannage, hilarious, unmissable, even on school nights. I was meant to be asleep long ago but, transistor radio under the covers, listened later than I should so we girls could laugh about his audacity next day at school! Happy days.
     Diana from Prestwich

***

In a live TV programme, comedian Jasper Carrot, on stage at the London Palladium, performed a routine describing how, when driving through Manchester following a gig, he had to stop his car and stare at his radio in disbelief at what was coming out of the speaker. Stannage would ask for listeners' views on a range of topics, from politics to sport, to the day's news or the monarchy, and then annihilate anyone who dared to have an opinion.

***

I used to listen to James Stannage as a child when I was supposed to be asleep. He used to make me laugh so much, as he was always horrible to everyone. When his first son was born (Darren, but I'm sure he told listeners that he was called James Darren), I wrote to Piccadilly Radio to congratulate him on the birth of his son. (Yes, an actual letter sent by post! Hard to believe now, isn't it!) James then read it out on air and was very complimentary about the letter. I felt so chuffed with myself that he'd actually been nice to me! I'm now sixty years old and it's still one of my fond memories.
     Regards, Caron

***

He would insult old ladies and sixth form students alike, calling them 'pillocks', telling them to 'get lost' because they were 'bloody idiots' or just to get off the line before he cut them off. It caused a storm and attracted huge listener numbers and media coverage. He was described as 'The man you love to hate'. Clearly, the Radio Authority had concerns but Walters, true to form, defended the programme and Stannage's performance.

So as not to overstep the mark with the now very excitable presenter, there would be a morning meeting to discuss how far he could go, limiting him to how many 'bloody', 'bollocks' and personal insults he could make. Eventually, Stannage would go too far off the rails and so was released from his contract. He did go back to Piccadilly some years later, but in a much more subdued style.

In hindsight, this was probably when the penny dropped about what would appeal to listeners. It became clear they enjoyed listening to personalities who understood what the region was about. They wanted a station that was lively, fun and which reflected their daily lives. Information, entertainment, and education yes, but with a certain style that was relevant and at times a bit off the wall. Your music *and* your friend.

Tony Emmerson was everyone's friend, on and off air, and is fondly remembered by colleagues and listeners, a great guy with a silky voice who did the night-time shift, handing over to the breakfast show. He was, however, a bit accident prone. Early one morning, the engineer in the workshop heard a record come to an end and then nothing, just the scratching of the needle going round and round and round.

He rushed to the studio, to be confronted by something resembling the *Marie Celeste*. A cigarette burning in ashtray, steaming coffee, but an empty chair. He rushed to check the toilets, the offices, the record library … but the building was empty. Then, from the direction of reception, he heard a childlike whimpering. Tony had gone to pick up the morning papers from the plaza and locked himself out of the building and was crying and shouting for someone to let him back in.

Another morning and another engineer was driving into the station and again, he heard a record come to an end and again … nothing. The engineer abandoned his car outside the studios and rushed into the studio to see Tony slumped in his chair, cigarette smoking, coffee steaming and thinks, 'Fuck, he's dead!' He ran panicking into the studio, whereupon Tony woke bolt upright from his deep sleep and gave a time check, as if nothing had happened.

Another night owl was the legendary presenter that was Mike Day, who regularly hosted *Night Beat* programmes each week, in 'the wee small hours of the morning'. To say that this didn't appear to give him a thrill and adrenaline rush is an understatement.

Standing about six foot seven inches tall, always in his cowboy boots, Mike cut an imposing figure as he strolled into the studio at about one minute to two for a 2am start to take over from Gary Davies or Dave Ward. In between taking control and playing a couple of tunes, Mike would invariably chat with the outgoing presenter and nine times out of ten, it was immediately obvious that he was very, very grumpy.

His demeanour rarely improved as the night wore on and you'd usually find him in the studio, sitting with his feet up on the desk, eyes closed, quite possibly having a quick snooze during a track, or he would be on the phone, off-air, to one of the regular *Night Beat* listeners who usually appeared to be sympathising with and counselling Mike.

The night-time producers found all this a bit perplexing, but the best bit always happened as the on-air track was coming to an end. Mike would suddenly rouse himself from his apparent slumber and draw the chair up the desk to reach out for the mic fader. And then, as if joined by some mystical connection, his face would break into an enormous smile as he opened the fader. He became Mr. Jolly for as long as the fader stayed open, chatting to callers, enthusing about the music and so on, but as soon as the segment was over, the smile disappeared as the fader closed. His facial muscles and that mic one fader must have had some umbilical link, it was astonishing. Then he'd usually utter some expletive, push back in his chair, and plonk his cowboy boots back on the desk.

***

Around the age of eighteen, I and most of my friends used to listen to Piccadilly day and night and visited the station to be on the Mike Shaft and Gary Davies shows.

My undying memory was late one night calling a phone in show. I spoke to the producer and they phoned me back and put me on hold until my time. I was tired but keen to make my call, so I waited.

The next thing I knew was that it was morning and time to go to work. The phone was still in my ear, so I just thought I never got on the show. On my way to work, however, I was listening to Piccadilly as always, and there was an advert for the show I'd called.

It went, "Listen to the evening show on Piccadilly Radio tonight between 10pm and 1am. This is what Andrew Fawcett of Mere thought about last night's programme."

Then there was the loud sound of me snoring! Clearly, I made the show after I fell asleep! So many people heard it and took the mickey out of me for ages!

Andrew Fawcett

***

John Clayton, who went on to run BBC Radio Lancashire, cut his teeth as a *Night Beat* presenter:

> It was a lot of fun, even if the music selection was dire as we had to play music we didn't have to pay for. Commercial radio's agreement with the Musicians' Union meant that stations were allowed nine hours of needle time in any twenty-four hours, the rest of the time had to be made up of live musicians or the playing of 'library' music.

That is, non-commercial music. One of the regular *Night Beat* musicians was a young student from Manchester's Royal College of Music, Howard Jones, who went on to have ten Top 10 singles in the 1980s:

> I could still tell you which tracks on those Arcade Benelux albums had become so worn out and scratched as to be unplayable. We had live musicians most nights, even if some of them appeared to be challenging Mike Day in the 'Who's the grumpiest person you've ever met?' stakes and we had the session tapes which had to be played as part of the commitment to the Musicians' Union agreement.
>
> *Night Beat* presenters also had to read the news! The last job for the newsreader on the late shift was to compile a bulletin's worth of reads that could go through the night until the early morning news person, Chris Moore, popped up with the 6am bulletin. A sheaf of yellow A4 would be delivered to the on-air studio in good time for the *Late Show* presenter to have a read through before presenting it at 1am and 2am and then handing it all over to the *Night Beat* presenter.
>
> That was the theory at least, but the plan never really took the legend that is Dave Ward into consideration (and more of him later). Dave didn't really do the news and would try to persuade anybody present to read the bulletin on his behalf. When there was no other option, he would go through the stories and immediately discard any of those where he felt he might struggle with either the pronunciation of, say, Russian leaders or for example, any story with a Welsh placename in it.
>
> It didn't matter about the significance of the story. Lead stories were frequently jettisoned because Dave didn't feel comfortable or confident that he'd get it right. Peak Wardy happened when he hit the news jingle and then just read the weather. All the other stories were in the bin! And as the person who often had to follow Dave, this meant that the first twenty minutes of my programme was spent rummaging through the bin to retrieve

the stories he'd chucked out and then trying to work out the order they were supposed to be in.

***

I was a teenager when Piccadilly came on air. I'd been into music since I was a little kid and, more importantly, I'd been a radio fan all that time too. The radio was on in our house all day from breakfast.

When I heard that we were going to get a local 'pop music' station in Manchester, I was very excited. I was twelve years old in April 1974, and from that day, Piccadilly was the ONLY station I listened to. I'd put it on when I got up to get ready for school, and when I got home, I'd put it on again. Like any self-respecting teenager, I used to listen in bed at night on a little earphone, so mum and dad wouldn't realise I was awake. I went to the roadshows and always hoped I'd win a t-shirt (never did); I rang in for requests (from a phone box as we didn't have a phone); I went to The Best Disco in Town; and of course, I came to the Plaza for stickers. So many stickers.

As my teenage years continued, I still listened every day and when I went to university in Liverpool in 1981, with a bit of experimentation with aerial wires and coat hangers, I could just about get Piccadilly at night, so I'd listen then whenever I could pick it up. Magic memories!

David Dunne

***

Chapter 6

First With News

It was really cool to work in the newsroom at Piccadilly. The nationals monitored our newsfeed because we broke big stories. It wasn't just news, it was 'Piccadilly News'. We owned it. When colleagues left, they went onto big things — Jane Beckwith, Piccadilly Radio journalist, 1980s

It was 1977.

The rings of Uranus were discovered.

Red Rum won a record third Grand National.

Star Wars opened in cinemas and became the highest grossing film of its time.

Virginia Wade won the centenary Wimbledon.

Elvis Presley died at his home in Graceland, aged forty-two; Marc Bolan died, aged twenty-nine; and Bing Crosby died, aged seventy-four.

The Sex Pistols released *Never Mind the Bollocks, Here's The Sex Pistols*.

Saturday Night Fever was released and became the biggest dancing movie of all time, catapulting the Bee Gees to newfound success.

Tommy Docherty was sacked by Manchester United following the revelation of his extramarital affair with the wife of the club physio. The Doc would become a regular presenter on Piccadilly.

And on Piccadilly Radio, Roger Day would broadcast non-stop for a marathon seventy-four hours, just for the fun of it …

***

The presenters may have got the fan mail and the adulation, but every single department at Piccadilly Radio was 'best in class' and none more so than the fabled newsroom, where talent was nurtured and investigative reporting actively encouraged. Genuine programming of excellence from a station that gave equal importance to its speech output as it did to the music that it played, the perfect solid foundations for its unprecedented commercial success.

The newsroom covered many major local and national events. The fire at Woolworths Piccadilly in 1979, which killed eleven people; the Moss Side riots of 1981; Pope John Paul the Second visiting Heaton Park in 1982, only a year after surviving an assassination attempt; a packed passenger jet bursting into flames at Manchester Airport in 1985, killing fifty-three passengers and two crew members; Alex Ferguson taking over as manager of Manchester United in 1986.

In those days, the newsroom was a highly pressurised working environment. There was no internet to check out stories; it was still very old school. Getting out and about in the Piccadilly Radio Outside Broadcast vehicle to report live from where the news was breaking; knocking on doors to speak to people who didn't want to speak to you; and working 24/7 when the news agenda demanded it.

Henry Matthews was one of the best known of the Piccadilly news readers, working at the station for over twenty years and reading thousands of bulletins in his time, his sonorous voice adding both gravitas and humour in equal measure as the story merited. It's fitting that he tells the story of how Piccadilly Radio was 'First with News', always:

> The challenge we faced was creating a credible news operation almost from scratch. Our listeners had to be able to trust us. Most of us were new to broadcasting, but we had to hold our own with long established news teams at BBC Northwest and Granada and, of course, BBC Radio Manchester, who had had a three-year start on us.

We also had to do it on the hour, every hour, and unlike our competitors, on the half hour in between. There was also our obligation to IRN - Independent Radio News - to keep the commercial radio network supplied with the news on our patch. They too, were engaged in a quest for credibility, in their case as a national news service.

We got wind that staff at BBC Radio Manchester had been told not to worry at the prospect of competition. Piccadilly Radio, they were told, would be 'little more than juke box radio'. They were probably not alone in such a presumption. But the gauntlet, having been thrown down, was picked up with a steely determination. We had to prove ourselves. And we did. Later down the line, we were to boast *Piccadilly: First with News, First with Sport*. But it was no boast!

Of course, no news operation can survive without news - and the news certainly co-operated. Looking back at that first decade or so, it is astonishing to recall how abundant it was. Not always good. More often than not, bad. But our mission was to report it. Accurately, honestly, fearlessly - and when circumstances demanded, compassionately.

The big story on the day Piccadilly Radio went on air was, not surprisingly, Piccadilly Radio going on air. We reported it confidently but modestly. We knew there would be more challenging days ahead. I aim here to give you a taste of the challenges we faced ... and how we coped.

The news didn't always take us far away from base. Mother Mac's was a back-street pub off Piccadilly, forever associated with a macabre mass murder. Our reporter, John Smithson, was quickly telling listeners how the disillusioned landlord had murdered his wife, three children and the cleaner, who just happened on the scene as he was preparing a funeral pyre. He then hurled himself on to the burning corpses, taking his own life too.

Barely a year later - and just a hundred yards away - an even greater tragedy unfolded. Seven young women began their evening shift in a top floor textile workshop on China Lane. An hour later, five were already dead, a further two were dying, trapped in a smoke-filled building while firefighters watched on helplessly.

Chris Moore had just taken over the bulletin desk after the lunch break, when someone from our front office told him there appeared to be a fire in a building across Piccadilly Gardens. Over the next few hours, Chris spearheaded our coverage of a fire at the Woolworth's store, with reporters feeding in graphic accounts of a desperate rescue operation from the scene.

Ten people died, most of them suffocated by thick toxic smoke from polyurethane fumes from blazing furniture. Firefighters rescued forty-seven people, all of whom required hospital treatment. It was the city's worst fire since World War Two and the fallout continued for weeks and months through inquests and an official inquiry.

At the end of one week in April 1980, a Friday mood had already arrived in the newsroom. In half an hour, the main shift of the day would be at an end and with it, for most, the working week. The atmosphere quickly changed, silenced by the almost inaudible 'ping' on our antiquated Press Association teleprinter. It was alerting us to what would prove our greatest challenge to date. Few of us there will forget 25 April 1980.

As duty editor, I watched with growing concern as the printer chattered away telling us a Boeing 727 aircraft which had left Manchester earlier that day was missing, overdue at its destination and originally feared to have come down in the sea. In fact, Dan-Air Flight 1008 had slammed into a mountain on its final approach into the notorious and regularly fog-shrouded Los Rodeos airport in Tenerife. All one hundred and forty-six passengers and crew perished.

It was the biggest disaster in our brief existence, the biggest story, too. The instant reaction of our then news editor, David Vere, was that we had to get to Tenerife. It was anything but simple, to get to the island by conventional means would have taken forty-eight hours. David decided it was time to call in a few favours, and so three hours later our fluent Spanish-speaking reporter, Nicola Meyrick, along with colleague Paul Newman, were heading out on board a private jet along with an ITN film crew.

At 7am on the Saturday morning - just thirteen hours after she had left the newsroom to race home for her passport - Nicola was filing the first of many reports from the crash scene, reports which for the following twenty-four hours were the basis of every news report of the catastrophe in this country, either in print or on the airwaves. We were the only British journalists there. Teamwork guaranteed the success of our coverage in the immediate hours after the accident and on the many days and weeks which followed, as air accident investigators sought an explanation for the crash. And credibility was never again an issue.

A similar effort was called for just five years later when another aviation disaster became top of our news agenda - this time much earlier in the day and much closer to home. At breakfast-time on 22 August 1985, a British Airtours Boeing 737 packed with holidaymakers bound for Corfu caught fire as it sped down the runway at Manchester Airport. Fifty-five people died, chiefly through breathing in choking toxic fumes. There were eighty-seven survivors.

There were so many strands to the story, only a team effort guaranteed it was brought to the air. That we succeeded was chiefly through the efforts of Trevor Green, our lead reporter on the story. Trevor covered every development in the days, weeks and months following the accident ensuring our coverage was the equal of, if not more authoritative than, most. It also led to his definitive documentary on the disaster which to this day remains the worst and only such disaster at Manchester Airport.

There was plenty of politics of course - but isn't there always. After just six months on air, we encountered our first general election. We had little to fear with Jim Hancock, our political and current affairs editor, masterminding our coverage. It was the first of six general elections between 1974 and 1992, reporting 'live' from all the counts in Greater Manchester, a tremendous collaboration between our news and engineering staff.

Our second, in May 1979, followed the collapse of the Labour government during the so-called 'winter of discontent', when we were tested to the full by an unprecedented series of strikes. Gravediggers in Tameside walked out meaning the dead went unburied; then the binmen struck leaving mountains of refuse uncollected; and hospital ancillary workers then joined in. The impact of it all on a conurbation of Greater Manchester's size was enormous. We had to keep pace with every development; listeners had come to rely on us.

Jim's task throughout two periods with Piccadilly was to navigate us through the complex world of politics and current affairs, first as presenter/producer of *Arena*, looking at a variety of social problems and featuring major interviews, and *Agenda* which covered local politics. Later, came *The World from the Northwest*. They were his programmes, bearing his own personal stamp.

Many high-profile figures came to know local commercial radio through Jim, who quickly dispelled any preconceived ideas that we might be mere lightweights in the game. Twice he interviewed Margaret Thatcher, first as a shadow cabinet member, then after she became PM, and Sir Keith Joseph used an interview with Jim to outline a radical change in government support for failing industries. His interviewees were those at the very heart of politics in the 1970s and 1980s - a formidable list including Ted Heath, Harold Wilson, Jim Callaghan, Michael Foot, Jeremy Thorpe and Oswald Mosley.

When we took to the air, controversy was raging over the efforts of Lord Longford to free the moors murderer, Myra Hindley, from her life sentence. The opposition to such a proposition was led in those days almost singly by Ann West, the mother of ten-year-old Lesley Ann Downey, one of the victims. The prospect these two protagonists could ever be brought together in a face-to-face confrontation on live radio looked extremely remote. But Ann had come to trust Piccadilly Radio in all our dealings with her and so it was that Jim brought them together, the result being sixty minutes of electrifying broadcasting. It had never been achieved before, nor was ever repeated.

Few colleagues envied his annual task, party conferences. They weren't everyone's idea of fun, though they were bread and butter to Jim. During the party conference season, Jim would be found in Brighton, Blackpool, wherever they were taking place, interviewing leading politicians. One year, it was decided to hire a small caravan to use as a mobile studio at the Lib Dem conference. In fact, it was so small that the (now disgraced) MP for Rochdale, Cyril Smith, couldn't get through the door as he was so fat and had to be interviewed outside.

Jim's competence as a 'hard news' man was tested to the full one morning in October 1984. This was unlike any other party conference before or after. Overnight, the IRA had attempted to assassinate the Prime Minister and much of the Cabinet with a bomb planted at the Grand Hotel in Brighton. They came perilously close to succeeding. Jim filed numerous reports in the proceeding hours, live linking our twenty-minute lunchtime news programme from the scene. Our coverage that day was on a par with that of any of our rivals. Juke Box radio, indeed!

Crime - serious crime - featured all too prominently on our daily news schedules, and it was crime which predominantly brought me to Piccadilly. Not long after going on air, the body of a teenage girl had been pulled out of the canal at Failsworth. Sharon Mosoph had been strangled; her body mutilated. She was the third victim of serial killer, Trevor Hardy, from north Manchester. His other victims, Wanda Skala and Janet Lesley Stewart, were also teenagers. We covered every development in a major investigation lasting some weeks, then every minute of the four-week trial at the conclusion of which the judge told Hardy: "This was a happy place - it will be a happier place still without you."

Piccadilly News formed a close relationship with the Mosoph and Skala families. They trusted us and with their co-operation and approval, we were able to give our listeners an insight into the anguish of two families whose lives were devastated by tragedy. The Hardy investigation led also to a close working relationship between Piccadilly Radio and our senior police officers, thanks to the influence of the man who led the Hardy murder inquiry. Detective Chief Supt. Tom Butcher, a vastly experienced cop and inspirational leader, was quick to acknowledge the immediacy of radio. He recognised he could be on air within minutes and appreciated just how valuable a tool it could prove to be in a criminal investigation. It was a point he impressed on many of his colleagues, which enabled us as a news team to do our jobs so much more effectively.

When the most infamous serial killer of all moved on to our patch we had to compete with the best. Indeed, on the night the Yorkshire Ripper, Peter Sutcliffe, was arrested, a tip-off from an impeccable source enabled Piccadilly to be among the first to break the story. It also sent me and Steve White, my colleague and an outstanding reporter, racing over the Pennines, the latest leg of a two-year journey that was to finally end a few months later in Court No. 1 at the Old Bailey. We were there for every day of the proceedings.

We didn't only cover death and mayhem, we covered life, too. A bizarre story was emerging from Oldham about work going on at a local hospital intended to result in what was called a 'test-tube baby'. It was a big story, why else would the world's press converge on, of all places, Oldham. *Time* magazine was there, so were *Paris Match* and *Bild, CNN* … and so was Piccadilly News.

For weeks, we competed with some top news teams, some fat cheque books and against an array of clever, if unorthodox tricks. Had we followed the lead of some Japanese photographers, we might have spoken to every pregnant woman spotted on the streets of the town. Or we might have been foolish enough and followed those *Paris Match* journalists who invested in a couple of white gowns to gain access to the maternity ward - only to be given away by their accents.

But no sooner, and no later, than any other news outlet, Piccadilly's Marion Bowman was telling listeners at breakfast time on 25 July 1978, that Louise Joy Brown had been born at Oldham and District General Hospital - the world's first test tube baby. Subsequently, the pioneering gynaecologist, Mr Patrick Steptoe, came into our studios and told me at length of the tortuous, but ultimately successful journey taken by him and scientist, Dr Robert Edwards, in their quest to end the misery of childless couples, by virtue of IVF.

For many, the journey to great accomplishments began on Piccadilly Plaza. I recall them - not in any pecking order.

Chris Bryer went on to Granada TV's award-winning *World in Action* before becoming head of documentaries at Yorkshire TV; John Smithson set up his own production company, winning a BAFTA for his documentary *Touching the Void* and is still making documentaries of the highest quality for TV worldwide; Jim Hancock went to the BBC's political unit in Westminster, before returning to the BBC in the Northwest as political editor; John Greenwood left for London and worked with BBC Radio London and teamed up with John Armstrong, another early staff member, at IRN.

Petrina Rance went to Yorkshire TV, as did Sita Guneratne, Petrina having the good sense to marry our programme controller Colin Walters and likewise, Sita, who became Chris Bryer's wife. Nicola Meyrick became editor of BBC Radio 4's highly acclaimed *Analysis* programme, then subsequently oversaw much of BBC Radio's current affairs speech output.

Paul Newman left to work for BBC TV in the Northwest, before joining TV-am, reporting live from the first Gulf War; Jan

Howarth left to teach radio journalism at London's City University and form an independent radio company; Chris Moore went to work for ITV News in the Midlands, before joining Sky News; Nik Pisani had a successful career, culminating as producer of BBC TV's *Question Time,* one of the top roles in current affairs television; Andrew Bomford left for Hong Kong and the *South China Morning Post*, before returning to London to work for BBC News.

Steve White was poached by the *Daily Mirror* - there could be no hard feelings as we had poached him in the first place - and became an associate editor of the paper; Jane Beckwith was lured back across the Pennines to Yorkshire TV; Joan Smith became a crime author and is now a book critic with the *Sunday Times*.

Stuart Flinders left, first for Granada, before finding his natural home at BBC Northwest, while Lesley Stevenson, who was to become his wife, moved on to make factual programmes for Granada. Jo Hartley, who married Trevor Green, left for a PR career handling all press relations for the Manchester Commonwealth Games, which she did with great distinction; Abigail Bonell left for a radio career in the United States - to this day hosting her own daily radio show.

There are those still hard at it. John Pickford is now Editor in Chief of Bauer Radio News. An innovative broadcaster, many of the features he pioneered and introduced as head of Piccadilly Radio's sports output are now common in radio and TV sports coverage nationally. And Paul Lockitt must be one of the most familiar voices on radio in Manchester and hereabouts, having been a news presenter at Piccadilly and now BBC Radio Manchester, stretching over several decades.

It was an enormous privilege and abundant pleasure to work with so many talented individuals - even now we look upon ourselves more as family than as former colleagues.

***

When you wanted to know what was going on in your area – the news, the sport, the weather, the traffic – Piccadilly was always the first choice. National radio stations didn't care what was going on north of Watford. You felt that Piccadilly was as much a part of the local community as you were. It was the friend that you'd want to go down the pub with.

    Pete Smith, Sale

***

You're up to date with the news ... Piccadilly Sport next.

Chapter 7

It's a Goal!

*Manchester's Piccadilly Radio used to pre-empt
the announcement of a goal from around the region
with a shrill "It's a goal!" if a local team scored.
Or an "Oh no!" if a team had conceded...*
— Andy Mitten, Manchester Evening News (October 2015)

It was 1978.

Nancy Spungen was stabbed to death in New York by Sid Vicious of the Sex Pistols.

The Bee Gees continued to dominate the charts with the soundtrack of the *Saturday Night Fever* movie.

Kate Bush's *Wuthering Heights* was released; and Rod Stewart asked, *Do Ya Think I'm Sexy?*

Viv Anderson became England's first-ever black player at full international level.

The Yorkshire Ripper continued his reign of terror.

GPS or Global Positioning System was developed.

The world's first 'test-tube baby,' Louise Brown, was delivered by Caesarean section at Oldham Hospital.

Illinois Bell Company introduced the first-ever Cellular Mobile Phone System.

And Piccadilly Radio knew *Grease* was the word. It was the big movie of the year, and on its UK premiere, Piccadilly Radio negotiated with the Manchester ABC cinema on Deansgate to buy the whole cinema and show the film at one minute past midnight on its opening day. VIP guests were invited. The station gave tickets to listeners who had to guess the mystery locations of hidden tickets.

***

One of the reasons for Piccadilly Radio's unprecedented success was its commitment to local sport. At the time, the Northwest was home to some of the best football teams in the country and listeners felt that the radio station was as fanatical a fan of their team as they were. The big three at the time were Manchester United, Manchester City and Bolton Wanderers and the very unbiased reporters covering those teams were Tom Tyrell, Brian Clarke and Matt Proctor. Stories of the 'Three Musketeers' could fill a book, but here are some of the best …

The Homecoming – Tom Tyrell interviews the Doc after United beat Liverpool 2-1 in the 1977 FA Cup Final.

For some reason, Tom Tyrell's press pass at Stamford Bridge for a Chelsea game against United wasn't valid, so he was refused entry. Fergie, as the story goes, smuggled Tom in, who then borrowed a primitive mobile phone and started voicing inserts from it. Standing next to him were a bunch of lairy Cockneys who realised what he was doing and started effing and blinding. A fight broke out. The stewards threw the lot of them out.

On air, 'We now go to Tom Tyrell who has been thrown out of the ground!' Tom had managed to find a gap behind the stands where he could see the ball in the air, and he made up a commentary, of sorts. Another steward realised what Tom was doing and stood in front of him to block what limited view he had. On air, it became far more entertaining for listeners to hear what was going on with Tom, rather than the game itself, a far cry from today's detailed analysis by broadcasters.

Tom Tyrell not only reported United games on air, but he was also the stadium announcer at Old Trafford. (The station also provided announcers at City and Oldham Athletic, amongst others.) Up there with 'Who shot JR?' was the *Coronation Street* cliff-hanger; 'Would Deidre Barlow go back to Ken, or run off with Mike Baldwin?' The nation held its breath. On the fateful night Deidre was due to make her decision, United were playing Arsenal in the second leg of the League Cup semi-final. Just before 8pm, AND DURING THE GAME, Tom announced to the crowd, "Here's a newsflash ... Deidre has decided to stay with Ken!" which was greeted with a huge cheer by the crowd. United went on to win the game 2-1 to get to Wembley, only to lose to Liverpool in the final.

Brian Clarke, 'Clarkey', was the Manchester City reporter. A lovely man, best described as a character. One Saturday, he had spent an entire afternoon drafting and updating scripts for both the sport bulletins and the half-hour *Talking Sport* programme, which was on air later that day. This was done on a manual typewriter in those days and when finished, the scripts needed several photocopies printed for other members of staff. This task was usually a job for the office secretary. However, one day, Brian had to do it himself. The photocopier, he was told, was out in the corridor, next to the industrial-sized shredder. Five minutes later, Brian returned to the newsroom, minus the scripts.

"The fucking photocopier's eaten the fucking scripts that I've been fucking writing all fucking afternoon!" he screamed.

"Did it make a loud grinding sound?" asked one of his colleagues.

"Fucking right it did!" he confirmed.

"That'll be the shredder then, Brian," came the reply.

Then there was the time Brian was covering a Salford rugby league game in the radio car. Typically, he'd forgotten the long cable drum, so he had to plug in to the dashboard and do his inserts from inside the car, which he'd parked near the corner flag to be able to see the game. In the closing minutes, somebody scored a try in the corner. Brian couldn't quite see what had happened, so he leaned forward to get a better view.

Unfortunately, Brian leaned on the horn. Because he had headphones on, he couldn't hear it, but the players could, and, thinking it was the hooter for the end of the game, they started walking off. Brian said, "This is extraordinary. The players are walking off. They think the game's over." Someone opened the car door and dragged him off the steering wheel, while the ref had to run after the players and tell them to restart the game.

One half time at a City game, Brian interviewed the legendary goalkeeper, Bert Trautman, who was there as a guest of the club.

"Tell me Bert, with having such a great career, was it frustrating that you never played an international for England?" he asked.

"Not really, Brian, I'm German," Trautman replied.

Brian's greatest coup as Piccadilly's City reporter was an exclusive he did with the Gallagher brothers. He was alone in the press box at Maine Road as Oasis were sorting out arrangements for their concert at the ground. They asked who he was and when told it was Brian Clarke, they asked, "Do you mean him from Piccadilly Radio?" When told it was, the brothers pleaded to be introduced to him. Never one to miss an opportunity, Brian recorded their chat and produced an hour long exclusive which went out nationally across the independent radio network.

Dave Ward and the legend that is Brian Clarke,
for years, the voice of the Blue half of the city.

Saturday Sport with James H. Reeve and Tommy Docherty was a compelling listen for so many football fans in Manchester. James, the passionate City fan, and Tommy, the former United manager, made for an entertaining pre-match and after-match phone-in. They were joined by Gary Owen, Peter Barnes, Paddy Crerand and Malcolm Allison who on one occasion, was picked up to do the show from (and returned to) the Priory, where he was receiving treatment.

Behind the scenes in the Master Control Room, it was always a cacophony of noise. Callers to the show were being vetted before being put through on air and match reporters were being monitored off air for their goals and match reports. Listeners were alerted to when goals were going in during the afternoon with "It's a goal!" and "Oh no!" and Piccadilly would bring full match commentary from an away match. The Doc would often host the phone-in from the press box of a football ground. Even when he had a brief spell as manager of Altrincham, he still managed to do the pre-match phone in from the station's radio car.

The show was so popular that one of Piccadilly's senior board members asked if he could bring in his two football mad boys to see how the show was produced. The production team were ordered to be on their best behaviour and the guests were intrigued by the spaghetti of wiring connecting the station to all the different football grounds and the delay system that ensured James H. could cut a caller off if they used a swear word or said anything defamatory.

Suddenly, there was a shout from one of the grounds: "Hello studio – we have an emergency - we are having to evacuate." It was the 'darling' of Oldham Athletic fans, Stuart Pyke, who was in the enclosed press box at Boundary Park. The producer turned up the volume on the feed from the ground and the boss and his sons leaned in to hear more. But the family made a hurried exit from the room and the radio station when the next part of the message boomed out: "Hello studio emergency – repeat emergency – the Doc has just farted and it is so bad we are having to evacuate the press box."

The red-faced boss was less than impressed as he ushered his sons out of the studio at speed.

"I think we've seen enough now," he said.

One day, the company secretary of Manchester United came into the station to accuse Piccadilly of breaking the broadcasting rules, thereby encouraging fans to stay away from home games. He was informed that the station adhered exactly to the rules of so many live updates.

"Ah," he said, "you don't. When there's a goal you shout, 'It's a goal!' Or 'Oh no!'"

It was pointed out to him that this was perfectly legal. He said, bizarrely, that it encouraged fans to stay at home listening instead of attending Old Trafford. This, of course, wasn't true, but there's no doubt that when people heard "It's a goal!" or "Oh no!" coming out of their radios, they stopped whatever they were doing and waited with bated breath to see if it was good news or bad news for their team.

***

While the brand doesn't exist anymore, the same as other local stations, the memory of Piccadilly Radio lives on and nothing will ever be the same as hearing those FM crackles, getting frustrated trying to listen to football on Saturday and hearing "It's a goal". Radio may be dead as we know it but long live Piccadilly!
    Caveman (Damon Carroll)

***

In his second stint as Manchester City boss, things weren't going well for Malcolm Allison. Results were poor and the pressure was mounting. "Should he go, or should he stay?" was the most debated question on all football phone-ins. Colin Walters came up with the idea of printing two car stickers, 'Mal must go!' and 'Stick with Mal!'. City fans could choose which one they wanted to display. (A pre-curser to premium phone line voting.) All went swimmingly with promotional girls offering fans the car stickers outside Maine Road at the next home game.

On *Match of the Day* that night, Jimmy Hill wasn't impressed. "Welcome viewers to *Match of the Day*, on the day that a local radio station in Manchester despicably produces stickers encouraging fans to try and put pressure on Manchester

City Football Club to sack Malcolm Allison!" Piccadilly was somewhat ahead of its time with regards to 'social media'. *Saturday Sport* had many presenters over the years, picked for their technical dexterity, rather than for their sporting knowledge. Often, there were six live games to link to, score flashes, ads to schedule, records to play and frantic producers talking incessantly in their ear. No one was better at working 'the controls' than Pete Baker, but he had no interest in sport whatsoever. Baker once announced the result of the 'Street Leger', rather than the St. Leger; gave the racing results from Towcester, reading it as it looked, rather than as it should be pronounced i.e., Toaster; and announced that Joe Jordan had scored for City, rather than United.

Simon Cole hosted the show for a couple of years and like Baker, it was more for the fact that he was a technical wizard, rather than a sporting guru. He recalls one less than impressive appearance:

> There was the South Africa Road incident where I, as a *Saturday Sport* presenter trying hard to cover for lack of detailed knowledge, used the Rothmans Football Yearbook every week to provide me with a crib sheet on teams / games / grounds. Of course, the book gave official stadium names which are sometimes not those used by fans. As I handed over to Richard Keys for the match preview of QPR's game against United at South Africa Road, there was a silence as Richard marshalled his thoughts for the put down, "Of course, it is probably more familiar to those who actually follow QPR as Loftus Road …"

Football players didn't get off-the-scale salaries in those days or earn huge amounts from image rights and sponsorship, so when teams reached a cup final it was expected that the media would contribute to the 'Players' Pool' for interviews pre- and post-final. United's Steve Coppell was responsible for collecting the monies from newspaper, TV, and radio (perhaps because he had a degree from Liverpool University in Economic

History). Also, Steve was one of the United and City players who recorded a 'Christmas Special', where they presented a show by themselves and chose their Top 10 records. United's Gary Birtles and City's Paul Power hosted shows, as did Gary Bailey, who was a natural and went on to become a national broadcaster back in South Africa. One Christmas, a fixture pile up meant that the station had to find a non-sporting celebrity to do the special. Bernard Manning was booked. After extensive editing, the show was ready to go out and a cheque for two hundred and fifty pounds was prepared to post to Bernard. When asked where he wanted it sending, he replied, "£250 quid! I don't want that. Use it to buy some toys for your Christmas appeal. But don't tell a fucking soul that I did that. I don't want people thinking I have a soft side."

First with Sport – Maine Road, derby day … we think.

Chapter 8

Presenters - The Golden Years

Radio is the medium for the introverted extrovert
— Terry Wogan

It was 1979.

Thousands of public and private workers went on strike in what became known as the 'Winter of Discontent'.

Sid Vicious, the former Sex Pistols guitarist, was found dead in New York after a heroin overdose.

Sebastian Coe set a record time for running a mile, completing it in 3 minutes 48.95 seconds in Oslo.

Manchester City paid a British club record fee of £1,450,000 for Wolves midfielder Steve Daley.

The first JD Wetherspoon pub was opened.

The first gay and lesbian civil rights march on Washington took place.

Margaret Thatcher became the first female prime minister of the UK.

There was the first recorded instance of a comet hitting the sun.

Piccadilly Radio's Roger Day performed a first with the Halle Orchestra in a different 'Final Night of the Proms'.

And after the longest strike in British television history, advertising agencies shifted the spending of clients' money onto radio. Charging 'top dollar', Piccadilly carried more advertising than usual, and did indeed become, 'a licence to print money'. The station was only allowed to make limited profit. As far as the excess money was concerned, Anthony Blond, said, "Give it to the staff!" They got a month's summer bonus and a Christmas one too.

***

It became clear to Colin Walters that the station was starting to develop its own personality, with audiences responding to a more irreverent, relaxed style of presentation and buying into the *First with Music. First with News* positioning, loving the very distinctive Northern emphasis.

The next phase would see the introduction and development of new presenters such as Phil Wood, Phil Sayer, Ray Teret and Dave Ward (who Pete Reeves would nick name 'Curly Shirley' and, before you ask, we have no idea why). Along with Andy Peebles and Roger Day, they would form a settled and very strong line up.

Rather than dedicated speech blocks such as *Piccadilly Central*, Roger Finnegan and Phil Griffin would present features, guest interviews and outside broadcasts throughout the daytime output, a style of programming that would develop creatively over time, with the introduction of programme producers. (More of that later.)

At the same time, Walters wasn't afraid to push the barriers and he introduced what at the time were very hard-hitting programmes, such as the first phone-in on sexual problems and the Family Care Line features, which would tackle issues such as incest and addiction, all of which no doubt made the IBA a bit nervous. However, these weren't programmes designed to shock, but to address topics that previously were taboo on radio, and the Radio Authority, in fairness, supported this pioneering approach.

Having made so much profit during the ITV strike, the station put forward ambitious programme ideas to the Radio Authority which could be funded from the secondary rental monies which otherwise would go back to the Authority.

Marion Bowman was sent to California to investigate what was going on in the newly created Silicon Valley and how microchips would soon be changing our lives. The result was a fascinating documentary, *Chips with Everything*. Marion also produced a programme on alcoholism, *Dying for a Drink*.

Roger Finnegan (right) and Abe Ginsberg (left)
interviewing … a barrel.

Producer Sue Carroll won a Sony Radio Gold Award with a hard-hitting documentary on male prostitution in Manchester, *Rent Boys*. Here was Piccadilly Radio beating Radio 4 at its own game.

And Brian Beech won a Sony Radio Gold Award for *My Generation*, a series of six half programmes dealing with teenage sexuality. He was presented with his award in London by Diddy David Hamilton and Roy Hattersley, MP.

These programmes would usually end with, "If you or your family members have been affected by what you've just heard, you can call the Piccadilly Family Careline for free, confidential advice." (This was a service that the station had set up and funded – way ahead of its time.)

Bear in mind that these programmes were aired in the 1970s ... on local radio! This was ground-breaking stuff and perfectly illustrate Colin Walters' pioneering approach.

Piccadilly Radio continued to go from success to success and the years 1979 to 1986 are considered to be its 'Golden

Years'. The presenter line up of Dave Ward, Susie Mathis, Mike Sweeney, Phil Wood, Timmy Mallett, Mike Shaft and Tim Grundy was known as 'The Magnificent 7'. Listening figures reached an all-time high of one and a half million; commercially, Piccadilly was the most profitable station in the UK; and it became a breeding ground of talent for broadcasters, programme makers and entrepreneurs.

***

As a ten-year-old growing up in Manchester, there was only one radio station. And that was Piccadilly. It was funny, cheeky, and relevant. Sexy Bexy and Curly Shirley woke us up every morning, had a seat around the breakfast table with the rest of the family and came in the car with us to catch the school bus. The breakfast show and its characters were woven seamlessly into our morning routine and are, along with the catchphrase "Curly Shirley - it's better than having your tonsils out," still remembered fondly forty years later.
   Charlotte Hickson

***

Dave Ward was one of the station's most popular presenters, much loved by listeners and colleagues alike. Think Clint Eastwood playing the sexy night-time radio DJ in *Play Misty for Me*. Then think again …

In his book, *It's Not What You Think,* Chris Evans encapsulates the presenter's appeal; 'Cuddly Dave was the late-night DJ who created a whole duvet-covered late-night world of intrigue and titillation throughout the bedrooms of the Northwest. He had the warmest of voices and a most alluring bedside manner. Never pervy, he somehow managed to attract what seemed like every single female who was listening to the show … while they were in bed! And on a weekday! Till two o'clock in the morning! They couldn't wait to talk to him. His show was huge, the girls listened because of Dave, and the boys listened because of the girls.'

Dave would turn up in the office to prep a couple of hours before going on air. He always had an attaché case – very trendy and professional at the time - which was always secured with a combination lock. He would go into the office, place his case on the desk and open it. You would expect a Filofax, files, posh pens, calculator but no, not Dave. He had his letters for that night's show, a hairbrush, his contact book, a Willy Warmer, a pair of lacy knickers and an eye mask. He would place these in his wire desk tray to take into the studio with him. When Dave set up his studio, he would have the Willy Warmer and knickers draped over the mic. So, when he referred to these, they were with him in the studio. When he said he was flashing his lights, his producer was at the dimmer switch turning them up and down. If he said he was sending you a hug, the mic got a hug. He lived every bit of that programme; you would have thought it was TV.

***

When I was ten, in 1977, our school entered a fireworks jingle competition where you had to write and perform a jingle that was no longer than a minute long and we won! We got to visit the station, meet one of the DJs and we all got given a 7-inch single. Then in 1982, I discovered Dave Ward's 'Under the Bedclothes' show from 11pm-2am, Sunday to Thursday, and listened every night (which is probably why I failed most of my O levels as I was too tired in school)! It was a brilliant programme with Easy Olive and Neville, who used to drive to different areas to see if listeners were flashing their bedroom lights on and off. I still have a tape recording of when he came to my area in Ashton-in-Makerfield. At 2am after it finished it used to be followed by a programme hosted by Gary Davies. I wonder what happened to him ...

John Clinton

***

***

Around 1980, I wrote into a slot which I think was called 'School and College Rock'. If your letter was selected, you were invited to go along with some of your fellow students and be part of the Gary Davies radio show. I was a fashion student at 'The Toast Rack' at the time. I strategically chose to write in on yellow paper, hoping that it would stand out and lo and behold, it did the trick. I wasn't particularly an especially big fan of Gary's smooth, medallion man image at the time, but I decided that a sartorial effort was required nevertheless and so I opted for spray on jeans, moon boots and a long fur effect charity shop coat with huge shoulder pads for the event. Along we went, full of student confidence and exuberance. When he came into the studio, I was quite suddenly 'star struck' and could only answer with a 'Yes' or 'No' to questions in the weirdest sounding squeaky voice, as my teeth had somehow stuck to my top lip with the enormity of his presence. Poor Gary, it must have been a very long, hard half hour or whatever it was.

My family were busy recording it at home with a little microphone next to the radio and were falling about at how bloody weird I sounded. I have met Gary since and on those occasions my top lip didn't Velcro itself to my teeth! He's a nice bloke and not a medallion in sight. As for me, the spray on jeans and shoulder pads are a very distant memory. It's HRT and 'Bargain Hunt' these days!!!
Sarah Eker

***

Having made his name on the late-night show, Dave was given the breakfast show, the most important slot on any radio station. His producer at the time, John Clayton, has very fond memories of those times:

> Working on the breakfast programme with Dave Ward and the motley crew known as the 'B' Team was always a joy. I'm not sure if the term 'zoo format' had been coined by then, but that's

what we had every morning. Everyone had a role to play, although the presenter occasionally forgot his! Following the publication of his best-selling book *Kicked into Touch*, ex-Manchester City apprentice and top Manchester office supplies magnate Fred Eyre had become a regular contributor to the sport output, and it was a no-brainer to draft him in to be the 'B' Team sport presenter.

Fred was always highly regarded for his dry wit and hilarious anecdotes which had made him a big draw on the sportsman's dinner circuit, so the idea was that he would add more than a soupçon of fun and mischief to the usual bulletins of score lines and groin strains. And like so many comedians, he needed a good stooge … but we gave him Dave Ward.

One memorable incident that summed up their relationship came the morning after the then Liverpool captain Kenny Dalglish had been injured in a midweek game. Fred knew only too well that the best ad libs are always rehearsed, so having prepared his script, he came into the studio well ahead of time to brief Dave: "So I'll say Kenny Dalglish suffered a fractured cheek in last night's game and you just chip in with 'Depressed?' and I'll say, 'Well, he's not very happy about it.' That Okay?"

As Dave's knowledge of football injuries and the like was somewhere between negligible and non-existent, Fred then went on to explain the concept of a depressed fracture of the cheek to make sure Dave properly understood the gag, before running it through with him at least twice.

But the best laid plans and all that. Fred duly delivered the promised line; "Kenny Dalglish suffered a fractured cheek in last night's game," at which point, bang on cue, Dave says, "Oh dear … and is he depressed about that Fred?"

Dave's actual age was one of the biggest talking points at the station. He could have been anything from eight to eighty! On an overseas trip (paid for by a record company), when Dave was required to show his passport, he refused to hand it to his producer at the check-in counter as it would mean he'd see his birth date which was, of course, one of Piccadilly Radio's greatest secrets.

***

Piccadilly Radio was most definitely the reason I became a fan of radio. I was born (not under a wandering star) just after 7am on October 10th, 1977. Within an hour, I had my first mention on the radio when my Nanna Ash (Mrs Dorothy Ashton of Bury) rang in for a song dedication. That song was the Jim Reeves classic 'Welcome to my World'. Of course, I have no memory of that moment, but my parents say it was Curly Shirley on the breakfast show at that point.

Years later, after my Nanna Ash passed away, I had the words 'Welcome to my World' tattooed on my arm as a homage to that moment (and my dear old Nanna), and every time someone asks me about the wording, my story always begins with, "Do you remember Piccadilly 261?" and thus, a conversation ensues … There will never be another station as good as Piccadilly Radio. We were truly blessed by quality across the Manchester airwaves.

Gareth Davies

***

And Dave's best ever link …

> Congratulations to Gladys, she's 111! Wow, 111, how amazing. Oh, she's ill, oops sorry, not 111. Get well soon Gladys.

In 1968, Susie Mathis, as lead singer of the Paper Dolls, had a top ten hit with *Something Here in My Heart (Keeps A Telling Me No)*. Despite no further chart success, the group toured widely and topped the bill at many venues on the UK cabaret circuit. Following changes in the line-up, the group disbanded in 1975. Under the name of Tiger Sue, Susie pursued a solo career and released three further singles.

After meeting Colin Walters in 1978, Susie began presenting various pieces into the daily (totally male-dominated) shows, live outside broadcasts from community events and, somewhat predictably, she became the weather girl for a time. Her experience in theatres and cabaret rooms meant that she was very comfortable in front of a live audience and with a memorable husky voice, coupled with a quick wit, Susie began to get noticed.

The next step was for her to present an hour-long lunchtime sixties weekday slot. After a career in front of live audiences, Susie soon learned that sitting in a studio just talking to a microphone was a totally different proposition, although she quickly adapted. She had no broadcasting experience, but was brimming over with personality.

In late 1980, audience research figures for the station dipped slightly for the first time since the launch. The drop was nothing major, but definitely a plateauing out. 'What would we do if they went down again?' was the question that was being asked. The big gamble was to promote Susie to mid-mornings and so, in early 1981, Susie became the first female on commercial radio to present a daytime show. Mid-morning shows had been and in many cases, still are, the preserve of male presenters. Appealing to a housewife audience at that time of the day was crucial and it was assumed that only male presenters could deliver.

Susie quickly blew that theory out of the water. With the support of producer Tim Grundy, her impact was immediate and not just with the female audience. A mix of celebrity guests, requests, and features such as Hands Across the Sea, where Susie reunited families who had lost touch through emigration with a long-distance call which listeners would listen in on! There wasn't a dry eye in the house and it was a long way from today, where we can talk to relatives in Australia live on WhatsApp.

Susie Mathis, once a singer with the Paper Dolls, became the first female to present a daytime show on commercial radio and deservedly, two years in a row, won the Sony Radio 'Local Radio Personality of the Year'.

Although the weekday audiences were great, the *Susie on Sunday* show became the most listened-to programme on the station. A mix of easy listening love songs, with 'Champagne and Roses' being sent to a deserving listener who had been nominated for doing something wonderful, along with the radio car visiting unsuspecting families, attracted huge audiences. At one point, a staggering three hundred thousand listeners tuned in during any half-hour during the three-hour show, an unheard-of number. Such was Susie's popularity that Pat Phoenix, who played Elsie Tanner on *Coronation Street*, chose to announce her retirement from the soap on 'my favourite radio station' during an exclusive interview on the *Susie Mathis Show*!

***

I would like to tell you about a wonderful experience I had back in 1982. I used to absolutely love listening to Piccadilly Radio 261. Every show was brilliant, but I especially loved Susie Mathis and Tim Grundy's show. My experience started when I entered a competition, on their show, to meet Sophia Loren! She was launching a perfume and there was going to be a launch lunch party held at the Piccadilly Hotel. The winner would visit the radio station and join the lunch, along with a friend, and get to meet Sophia Loren. The runners up would receive some of the perfume. I was so excited to hear the winner being drawn on their show, although I was one of the runners up. But then the winner said that his partner would not be able to join him for some reason. Susie suggested that maybe he would like to invite one of the runners up to join him on the day. To my joy, he chose my name!

On the day I was scheduled to be collected, I was getting ready and listening to the radio and heard Susie say that the car was on its way to pick me up! Low and behold, a Rolls Royce (can you believe it) arrived and waltzed me off to meet Susie and Tim! To be honest, my day was made then! But then I was taken to enjoy the lunch with Susie and the winning entrant. I remember he had brought some roses to give to Ms Loren. After the lunch, she came and sat at each table for a quick chat and signed my menu. She was beautiful, but I was quite star-struck and couldn't really speak to her. I have never forgotten the day, but meeting Susie and Tim was the very best part of it!
Julie White

***

Susie would regularly ask listeners to call in with their take on the celebrity gossip columns and trashy stories were discussed, as well as listeners' views on the latest soap opera story lines. (Sound familiar? Remember Anthony Blond's ideas in the original submission.) One Sunday morning, a caller working in a bakery came on air with the most over-the-top, hysterical commentary on some story or other. No one can remember what it was about and besides, it was irrelevant, because the station had unearthed another star. Welcome Umberto Saoncella, a funny, clever, larger than life, unashamedly camp character who, after being a perfect foil for Susie, would become a major presenter in his own right, especially when teamed-up with Dave Ward on Piccadilly Magic's breakfast show some years later.

***

I remember being around fourteen and wrote a poem about my mum. I sent it to Susie Mathis for her Sunday morning show, 'Champagne and Roses'. It was a Mother's Day competition and I won it for my mum. I was absolutely made up.

Also, my late brother Andrew would ring Umberto on his show. Poor Umberto could never get him off the phone.

It was a great station. Something for everyone. I can still remember the smell of the adhesive on the 261 window stickers.

Great childhood memories!

Regards, Julie Dolecki

***

So, the gamble on Susie had paid off, and she deservedly won the Sony Radio 'Local Radio Personality of the Year' two years in a row. Now, if that was a gamble … bring on Mike Sweeney. As mentioned previously, on occasion the route into radio was a less than traditional one. Dave Ward had been a hairdresser, Susie Mathis a singer with the Paper Dolls and one of its highest profile presenters, Mike Sweeney, a van driver.

***

Yes, yes! We all had Radio 1 and the Top 40 every Sunday, but Piccadilly Radio was our local station and we loved it. Steve Penk, Dave Ward, Phil Wood, Sweeney, Gary Davies and Umberto just to name a few, became our regular listening. My best memory of it was being fourteen/fifteen and at the Piccadilly Roadshow in 1980 at Salford's rugby ground. Hot sunny day, hanging with my mates, £2 a ticket, meeting all the DJs and then having music from The Trend, Salford Jets and The Dooleys. It was a long day and my first live music event, and I absolutely loved it. From then on, it shaped my love for live music gigs and that's still ongoing! Thanks 261.
    Lesley Boardman

***

"SWEEN-EY!!!"

Tony Ingham explains how a bloke from Salford became one of the best-known voices on radio:

One day, Colin Walters comes into my office with a cassette. "Have you heard this interview from the Salford Rugby Club Fair last weekend with a bloke called Mike Sweeney?" It was different! What an accent, so I got him in for a chat. I also went to the Duke of Wellington pub on Bolton Road in Swinton the following Monday to watch Mike as lead singer with his band, Salford Jets. It was rammed. The band were good, but in between songs, Sweeney was mesmeric, very, very funny. I got him in for an audition. It's raw, but it worked, and I gave him a Sunday evening slot for a few weeks where he couldn't do any damage. Quickly, there's a bit of a buzz.

Around that time, the RAJAR results came in – the research into audience figures - and it wasn't good news. The station wasn't really pulling up trees with anything innovative at this time and we clearly needed to freshen things up even further. Rather than wait and see if audience figures stagnated, Colin decided to go for it. We replaced Ray Teret with Sweeney and 'BOOM!' We entered the most successful period, in audience terms, the station ever enjoyed. Figures went through the roof. So, I tell Sweeney - who is at the time driving a van on £50 a week - what's going to happen and offered him £250 a week for five two hour shows. The next day, he tells me that his band mates are worried that this might affect the future of the band and would I talk to them!

They came in at 8pm one night the following week and asked for reassurances that this new daytime show wouldn't interfere with their musical ambitions. I tell them that we don't even know if it will work and as long as Mike turns up for his shows, he can do what he wants, but the future of Salford Jets was not my problem. So, after having been persuaded to give this radio malarkey a go, Sweeney was let loose on air.

With such a distinct Salford accent and a jack-the-lad attitude, it was decided to throw the broadcasting rule book out of the window. No Piccadilly jingles for Salford's 'hard man'. Instead, his lunchtime show opened with the intro to the Sex Pistols' *Pretty Vacant*, followed by a screaming 'Sweeney!' Here was a presenter who refused to play ABBA, instead played Bruce Springsteen and Elvis (but only before the King joined the army because that's when he sold out according to Mike), interspersed occasionally with the Singing Nun's *Dominique* and *How much is that doggy in the window?* Somewhat different to say the least and sometimes off the scale ... but boy did it work.

***

I worked at an advertising agency on Castlefields and we had Piccadilly Radio on all day, but our favourite part was listening to Mike Sweeney's 'Dead good, dead hard quiz for growny uppy people.' I loved Umberto too and I still have a Certificate of Participation from Suzie Mathis and a signed photo of Noddy Holder sent with a prize from a competition I won. Best radio station ever!
    Michelle Leversedge

***

Mike's distinctive voice was so instantly recognisable that every time he went out recording interviews, his producer just knew that it would take twice as long as expected. Fortunately, it was usually people wanting an autograph, a quick chat about 'United' or simply to shout, 'Have you got any ABBA?' and only occasionally, were diplomatic, peace-keeping skills required. For producer John Clayton, it was something of a welcome change to be offered the opportunity to go somewhere where Mike wasn't so well known or even known at all. Somewhere like, say, Paris, where they were invited by CBS records on an all-expenses trip to interview Mick Jagger about his forthcoming solo album, *She's The Boss*. As John remembers:

We'd been allocated a whole ten minutes with the Stones' frontman but sitting in a basement studio in CBS Paris, Mick and

Mike really hit it off and we ended up with the best part of an hour on tape. I'm still one hundred percent certain that Mike's opening gambit was something along the lines of, "Let's talk about all those drugs you used to take in the 60's", but whatever he said, it was one of Mike's best interviews. Job done, we celebrated with a beer or two, let CBS treat us to a slap-up meal in a very swish Parisian restaurant and then the next day, boarded the flight back to Heathrow. For the best part of two whole days, not one person had bellowed "Sweeeney" in our faces, there hadn't been a single mention of Abba and amazingly, Mike hadn't antagonised anyone just by being Mike.

Once on board, however, we discovered that every member of the crew was a Manc and a listener too, but the plus side to this meant that we were treated as first class passengers with champagne and a visit to the flight deck to meet the captain. After a brief chat and a couple of autographs, Mike, who isn't the world's greatest traveller, indicated that we should return to our seats, but as we left the cockpit, who should be sitting in the front row of the first class but … Mick Jagger, who immediately said, "Hiya lads!" Mick recognised Mike! Now that IS fame.

***

One of my best memories as an early teenager was listening to Tim Grundy on the 11pm – 2am slot. I loved the 'Stop the Clock' adventures. I'm hoping I've remembered that right. Where callers had to guess the location of the roving reporter (was she called Rita??) based on time limited clues. I listened to this via a Sharp music centre. One of those pieces of equipment about the size of a suitcase that had a combined turntable, cassette deck, and radio. The FM radio never worked until one day, I learned that I needed an antenna for it. Cue a trip to Maplins. Once I plugged it in, I was astonished at the quality of the sound compared to the crackly old MW. I had to listen through headphones as there was no way I was allowed to stay up this late on a school night. In a dark bedroom wearing PJs, with a cover over the lights on the music centre and wearing headphones, I looked forward every night to the Tim Grundy show.

To this day, I don't know if the roving reporter actually went to the places. At the time, I thought it was fantastic how she got to somewhere different every day. Later in life, the thought struck me that she might easily have been in the studio next door reading clues out of a travel book overlaid with sound effects to make her sound local to the place she was. Please don't ever tell which it was. I want to believe the romantic idea that she really did travel here, there, and everywhere. It's a memory of days gone by when things like adventure, programming, and entertainment were all possible before the accountants fully stepped in looking for ways to do everything on the cheap.

Remembering this has made me smile a huge amount. Thank you, Piccadilly.

And 'Thank You' Tim Grundy. He's a very nice man, a very nice man, a very nice man indeed. A sad loss to the world.

Steve Douglas Park

***

It was almost inevitable that Tim Grundy would follow his father, the legendary Bill Grundy, into broadcasting. He'd started as a producer at Piccadilly, winning awards for interviews with high profile celebrities and for *The Ticking of the Clock* about Rolls Royce (the ticking of the clock, apparently, being the only thing, you can hear in a Rolls Royce when it cruises at sixty miles per hour), before becoming a daytime presenter.

Together with his producer, Tim came up with a week-long series called *Walking the Pennine Way,* which would see them travelling across a week from the start of the Pennine Way in Edale to a point about halfway along the route in North Yorkshire, but which, in reality, would involve them doing pretty much no walking whatsoever.

Pete Johnson was the technical supremo in the Outside Broadcast truck and the plan was to present the mid-morning programme from five strategically located Webster's and Wilsons pubs. Based in Halifax, the brewery had pubs throughout the areas Tim was passing through, so they very generously agreed to sponsor the project and furthermore, supplied the team with plenty of product to enjoy on the way. They were to be joined by a plethora of stars and celebrities and several Piccadilly colleagues also joined in on different days. But if they did actually walk on the Pennine Way, it could have been for no more than a hundred yards or so. The rest was a figment of the imagination because they were busy recording interviews and features at places near to the route … and consuming all that lovely free beer!

By Wednesday, the travellers had reached Haworth, the epicentre of Bronte country. At this point, they had been joined in their mission by fellow presenter, Mark Radcliffe. Haworth is a lovely little village with its cobbled Main Street leading up to the parsonage where Charlotte, Emily and Anne Bronte lived, along with their brother Branwell. While the sisters achieved lasting fame for their writing, Branwell didn't and the clue for why this didn't happen is right there on Main Street which certainly at the time Tim and the team were there, was home to rather a lot of public houses, every one of which appeared to bear a plaque proclaiming that Branwell Bronte had been a regular there. And so it was that after editing all the pre-recorded interviews for the next morning's programme, the happy band decided that they should drink a pint in every pub that Branwell Bronte had frequented, which was a lot.

No one who was there remembers how much they all had to drink that night, but it seems that Tim was completely out of it by the end. The following morning, he didn't appear for breakfast and the producer realised that he was in danger of missing the agreed hook-up with the breakfast programme at 8.15am, so he dashed to Tim's room and found him soundly asleep in bed. He just about managed to wake him, get him dressed and drag him out of the room, even though he was still half asleep and still clearly under the influence.

This was, of course, before mobile phones, so the call had to be made from a public phone box outside, and therefore, it was the producer's job to manhandle a corpse-like Tim into the street and then prop him up against the call box while he dialled the station. Once connected, Tim was shoved into the box and the receiver pressed into his hand. Somehow, he managed to sound vaguely coherent for about thirty seconds, but it wasn't the greatest bit of broadcasting the world has ever heard. Once he'd hung up, he went back to his room, where he promptly fell asleep again.

As the links for the first forty-five minutes of the programme were already recorded, all the team were pretending to be walking that morning into Haworth and it was decided to let Tim sleep it off, as long as someone could go back to the B&B by 10.30am to get him to the outside broadcast site. This excellent plan had just two flaws; firstly, the OB was in a pub that was opening early especially for the team and as anyone who has ever been in a pub in a morning will tell you, that distinctive aroma that is so welcome in the evening can be stomach-churning for even the strongest constitution and utterly nauseous for anyone who overdid it the night before. Secondly, the Tim that had recorded the "Good morning, here we are on the way to Haworth" pieces the day before had been sober, jolly, and upbeat, full of the joys of spring, so goodness knows what the listener must have thought when the live, 'morning-after-the-night-before' Tim eventually appeared on-air in some crazy Jekyll and Hyde transformation of the worst possible kind. He could barely string two words together, never mind a whole sentence and as if that wasn't bad enough, the head man from the brewery was treating the team to lunch after the programme. This was in a different pub, but when they arrived at this venue, Tim was still struggling, so he had a snooze in his car while everyone else schmoozed with our sponsor. Tim didn't touch a drop of alcohol for the rest of the week.

***

I listened to Piccadilly Radio all the time. I remember 'Underneath the Bed Clothes' with Dave Ward. I had a kiss with him in the Arndale when he did his sponsored kissy thing. I used to like the Mike Sweeney show as it was funny, and he played great music.

However, my best memory is going into the studio late on a Sunday evening to play a game on the Tim Grundy Show, think it was called 'Where in the World am I?' I was in the studio and guests had to phone in with clues to suggest whereabouts you were. If you guessed wrong the money went down, think it started at £50. Anyway, the answer to my question was Spandau Prison and I won £40 which was a good amount of money back then.

One of my greatest memories about that night was the fact that I have Reynauds and my fingers were frozen at the time. Tim took me to the vending machine to get a hot drink and I promptly stuck my fingers in my brew just to warm them up. Ha ha - got such strange looks! Happy days.

Pauline Murphy

***

After Andy Peebles' departure, the search was on for a replacement. Mike Shaft was a very successful soul DJ on the Northwest club circuit and although he had no radio broadcasting experience, he was an obvious prospect. As coincidence would have it, a Radio 1 Northwest producer, Tony Hales, had spoken to Mike with a view to him joining the station, but was waiting for the right opportunity and budget to appoint him.

After being interviewed by Walters a couple of times, Mike was offered the chance to replace Peebles, but with a proviso, Walters wanted him to drop the Shaft stage name. So here was Mike's dilemma: jump at the chance to be Piccadilly's next 'Soul Man' or hold out to see if the Radio 1 possibility came to fruition. Based on 'A bird in the hand is worth two in the bush', Mike accepted the Piccadilly offer, but steadfastly refused to change the name on which his reputation had been built. He could be very headstrong, could Mike.

However, he did change the programme's name from *Soul Train* to *Taking Care of Business* and it quickly became one of the most popular shows across the Northwest and beyond. Mike would invite club DJs into the studio to talk about what was happening musically in their area; he also introduced mixes to the show, which had never been done before; and he attracted a whole band of celebrity fans. Manchester United striker, Mark Hughes, once asked Tom Tyrell, head of sport, if he could get a copy of the previous Sunday's mix as he had been unable to record it!

As head of music, Mike would choose what new music Piccadilly would play – he could pick a hit, no problem. But … he was very principled! When Soft Cell's *Tainted Love* came out, he didn't put it on the playlist. After a week or so, he was asked why not.

"It's not as good as the original by Gloria Jones," (a song from the 1960s), he said.

"So???" came the reply.

"I'm not playing it," he confirmed adamantly.

The second biggest selling hit of 1981 - over a million sales and still considered a classic - Piccadilly never played the new version. To this day, Mike still thinks he was right!

Mike's very successful radio career continues today. After leaving Piccadilly, he won the radio franchise which saw him create and run Sunset Radio, which during its relatively short life was a very popular black music station. And in 2017, Mike's Radio Manchester show won the national Jerusalem Award – it being recognised as having 'a delightful presentational style and truly fitting of the great city from which it comes … willing to ask any question and to leave questions open, this is 21st century religious broadcasting.' A great guy and a great broadcaster.

Mike Shaft, still taking care of business after all these years.

Phil Wood, he of 'Put some more Wood on the Wireless' fame, was one Piccadilly's original presenters, but it wasn't his chosen career path. He was working for an advertising agency and for several years ran his own mobile disco, the Woodpecker, in his spare time, as well as doing regular sessions in local clubs.

A club owner called Phil and asked him if he had seen an advertisement in the *Manchester Evening News* inviting people to apply for jobs as DJs/presenters on a 'soon to be launched independent radio station – Manchester's first.'

The club owner also offered Phil a few words of advice that were to prove invaluable. Phil recalls:

He said that if I intended to apply, I should record a demo session and have it ready as that would be the first thing they would ask for. He invited me to record it at his club and just as he had predicted, a call came in response to my initial application asking for just that.

A seemingly endless series of interviews, with a succession of more senior executives, culminated with a meeting with 'the big boss', Philip Birch, the entrepreneur founder of Piccadilly 261.

He was a tall, imposing figure of a man, just as I imagined the captain of the QE2 might be.

Phil was soon to receive the all-important call. The receptionist at the advertising agency, now accustomed to taking the series of earlier calls to Phil from the same source, announced loudly, "Phil, it's that man again! He says it's very important."

My father didn't think it was a good career move but said that if I really wanted the job I should take it, as I would only regret not giving it a go if I didn't.

Quickly establishing himself as one of the new station's top presenters, Phil was soon mixing with top stars of that period. Having a genuine passion for Latin American music, Phil was thrilled when a new record arrived in his post box one day featuring a little-known Spanish singer, Julio Iglesias. *Begin the Beguine* was reminiscent of summer holidays, warm evenings and good times. Phil loved it and played it to death! The audience also loved it, to the extent that Piccadilly Radio was credited with introducing Julio to the UK market and playing a major part in creating a national number one record for him. Phil continues:

He [Julio] and his publicists were so grateful for our support that when he came over to promote his first UK tour, they agreed to just two one-to-one media interviews … one with me, and the second with a certain Michael Parkinson. When I met him, I found him to be a lovely fella, a real charmer. On the day, the studio was rammed with press, security and <u>all</u> of the station's female staff. For three years after our meeting, Julio sent me and my family a personal Christmas card from his home in Florida.

Phil was always an innovative broadcaster and he and his producer came up with an idea of the 'Top Ten' something or other. Listeners, for example, had to guess the top ten Heinz soups in order and the prize was free soup which Heinz agreed to supply. One day, Security called Phil's producer to tell him the soup had arrived in the loading bay. He discovered that they had sent ten pallets of the stuff, ten tons of tomato soup! Listeners were asked to come and collect their prizes, which of course they couldn't, so Phil and his producer Pete Johnson had to take hundreds of tins home. Pete says he's still finding tins of mulligatawny soup under his bed to this day! They then tried it with the top ten wines and crisps and anything they fancied, until the radio authority stepped in and stopped this 'Free advertising'.

***

So many happy memories. Under the bed clothes with Dave Ward. Mike Sweeney, the fabulous Susie Mathis and Dave Ward. But the best of all – 'Put a Bit of Wood on the Wireless' - the amazingly entertaining Phil Wood.

I won tickets to see Elton John in Leeds Queens Hall for the I'm still standing tour. "You've got the best seats in the house and luxury travel from Manchester to Leeds," he said.

All tickets were standing only, and we got a coach from Chorlton Street. Luxury enough for me! And I won a 261 t-shirt at the then Manchester Show. I wore it with pride!

Paula Borowiak

***

Colin Walters called Phil the most nervous presenter in the world, but when Phil took over the breakfast show, he was more popular in the Northwest than Noel Edmunds who was on Radio 1 at the same time. Phil remembers the sheer madness of it all, trying to make his show as original as possible, with potty characters and asking the audience to do barmy things … which fortunately they loved to do! As Phil remembers:

> There was *The Piccadilly Code Call*. You would only get about four rings to answer, using the most ridiculous code which would deliver the prize! "Now then how doo, would that be PW calling me to enquire as to whether my truffles were being grooved or not?" The call was nearly always answered correctly!

> One of my favourite elements of the show was the selection of crazy characters that peppered every morning's madness. Daphne the receptionist, always inebriated, with a major hearing problem. A memorable time was when she interrupted the show to tell me, (she thought I was the promotions department) that Roger Day was in reception. "No rush, he's only been waiting fourteen days. He's complaining about a Piccadilly t-shirt he's bought here in reception. IT'S SHRUNK! He says he's only washed it seventy-three times! Should I give him a sticker lovey?"

> Another regular was the PR Chief of The Transylvanian Tourist Board, Count Dracula. He would often call the show to highlight his latest discounted deal, designed to attract prospective tourists to the delights of the Carpathian Mountains. As ever, it was always some thinly veiled wheeze to entice easily led types into his lair, whereafter the visitors dined on a few cheap sandwiches, The Count and assistant Igor then dined on the visitors. All good fun, with plenty of thunder crashes, lightning strikes, screams and bags of bats in the belfry.

We should also mention other presenters who began their careers on Piccadilly, but who would make their mark later. Steve Penk was only sixteen years old when he joined the station. Like so many others, he would begin at a junior level, learning his craft doing various jobs. He first started to realise his potential when he presented a Saturday evening *Piccadilly Magic* show featuring classic hits. This was the start of a broadcasting career which slowly blossomed, and which eventually would result in him becoming the incredibly popular breakfast show presenter on Key 103. His 'wind-up' calls on unsuspecting listeners would become legendary and eventually, see him move on to national radio stations. Sixteen years old! Can you imagine that happening today?

James H. Reeve initially joined the station in 1976 as yet another broadcast assistant answering phones and taking dedications from listeners, and logging all the records so the writers and performers got their royalties. (The 'H' stood for Hengist and he used his middle initial in order not to be confused with the dead American country and western crooner, Jim Reeves!) He drifted into the Features Department and for a while, presented a double-headed early evening phone-in with Colin Walters which was once bizarrely featured in *Woman's Own*.

In 1979, Manchester's Victorian sewers started to collapse at an alarming rate. In a twelve-month period, over forty-nine holes appeared in the city centre causing massive disruption. The ever-inventive James H. suggested a competition based on 'Spot the Ball.' His idea was to print a map of the city centre and ask listeners to mark where they thought the next hole would appear! The station didn't do it … but it should have!

James's Piccadilly career was, to say the least, a bit odd. He got fired at least once, left and came back at least twice, never really finding his place until 1985 when he started to front the 10pm to 1am phone-in, which he did for three years. He would eventually team up with Dave Ward on the Piccadilly Magic 1152 Breakfast Show, as well as presenting Saturday Sport with Tommy Docherty for eight years and he became another hugely popular presenter who started on Piccadilly.

James H. Reeve. Not to be confused with
American crooner, Jim Reeves.

Becky Want joined Piccadilly Radio in 1984, having been a
secretary at Stoke's Signal Radio where Tony Hawkins, a
Piccadilly old boy, let her do a one-hour show on a Sunday
afternoon. After much persistence, she was offered *Nightbeat* a
couple of times a week at Piccadilly by Simon Cole, before she
got her big break and became part of Dave Ward's 'B' Team,
where 'Sexy Bexy' was born. Becky eventually took over Susie
Mathis's afternoon show and became one of the station's most
popular presenters. In 1988, she launched Key 103 with Tim
Grundy, before a career in television saw her host such shows

as *Granada Tonight, What's New, Travellers' Check* and *Inside Out*. She's still broadcasting on BBC Radio Manchester presenting the show after … Mike Sweeney!

And another presenter whose career began on the station was Stu Allen. Originally cutting his teeth on the overnight 'graveyard' shift, Stu took responsibility for the soul show when Mike Shaft left in 1986. He introduced dance music into the format and very quickly, led the way in promoting dance and rave music to the airwaves. His reputation grew when the station became KEY 103 and he is quite rightly acknowledged as a true pioneer of the genre. Sadly, Stu passed away in September 2022.

***

The legend that was Stu Allen definitely deserves a mention in the book. Along with eight thousand people, I danced in his honour a few months after his passing as a memorial to him. We all started listening to his music on a Sunday evening - his show was amazing every week. You can't write a book about the station without including how awesome Stu Allen was.

Emma Feetham

***

I started listening to Stu Allan's late-night show when I was around eleven years old, in my bedroom on my radio alarm. I'd originally started listening because I knew him as a child, and I thought I'd see what his show was like. It was like nothing I'd ever heard before and at first, I thought 'These are really long songs', but as I kept dipping in and out of the show, I realised that they were different songs, and he was mixing them together. This was dance music and I loved it. That show set me on a musical journey, which I'm still on now, thirty-two years later. He introduced me to a genre of music that I'd never heard before, but it blew my young mind. I saw him DJ many times over the years at Bowlers, but it all began on that radio show. I know thousands

of others who could share a similar story about Stu and that show. He was a pioneer and a true innovator of the dance scene.
   Tina Clarke

***

Chapter 9

Behind every Presenter ...

Radio is the theatre of the mind;
Television is the theatre of the mindless
— Steve Allen

It was 1980.

Granada's *TV World in Action* accused Manchester United's chairman, Louis Edwards, of illegal payments.

Pink Floyd's album *The Wall* hit number 1.

Blondie released their single *Call Me*, which would become the Billboard Song of the Year 1980.

Ian Curtis, the singer-songwriter of acclaimed band Joy Division, was found hanged at the age of twenty-three.

Photographer Annie Leibovitz had the last-ever photoshoot with John Lennon

The Rubik's Cube made its international debut at the British Toy and Hobby Fair, Earl's Court, London.

Post-It-Notes were first introduced.

Work began on ENQUIRE by Tim Berners-Lee leading to the World Wide Web's launch in autumn, 1990.

A record number of viewers watched the U.S. television show *Dallas* to discover who shot J. R. Ewing.

The ship that housed pirate radio station Radio Caroline, the *MV Mi Amigo*, sank off the coast of England.

Piccadilly Radio promoted and recorded concerts with national and international artistes at venues across the Northwest. *Magic of the 60s* nights were sold out within hours. Every genre of music was showcased.

***

As the Piccadilly sound started to formulate, the station began to develop its own style in terms of integrating speech into the music-dominated output, rather than 'programmes' as such. Interviews with celebrities, outside broadcasts, competitions and regular features would be spread throughout the day. To facilitate this, producers were introduced to work with the presenters.

In what was becoming a trademark unwritten recruitment process, the producers came from quite diverse backgrounds, the main criteria being, 'Do they get it?' and 'Are they one of us?' Looking back, it's quite remarkable that so many of those young producers (all in their twenties) not only made a telling contribution to the station's popularity, but later went on to have very successful careers in other fields.

Roger Finnegan was given a producer's position at Radio Nottingham by Colin Walters. (The only other job he applied for after university was as a warden in a donkey sanctuary. He didn't get that …) Meanwhile, as mentioned previously, after staff at Radio Nottingham had been sent an intimidating memo by Walters warning them that if they applied for a position at one of the new commercial stations, they would be sacked, Walters himself then soon left to join Piccadilly Radio. Then, he poached Roger Finnegan and Stephen Beard from Radio Nottingham to run Piccadilly Radio's Features Department.

Finnegan was one of Piccadilly's most talented programme makers. He left the station in 1979 to become San Francisco correspondent for Independent Radio News. While there, he made a documentary for Piccadilly called *An 8.3 in Business Hours* about the threatened California earthquake, which was a runner up in the prestigious Sony Awards. In 1981, Finnegan returned to the UK as a reporter for *File on 4* on Radio 4.

He remembers his time in Manchester with much affection:

Colin Walters could administer the hairdryer treatment or sometimes, often unexpectedly, put his arm around your shoulder. Very occasionally, he combined both techniques. As a young and sometimes barmy twenty-five-year-old, I often misbehaved, sometimes in a Piccadilly Radio branded vehicle. On one occasion, I'd been out in Bolton doing an interview. In the passenger seat alongside me, I had a Second World War German helmet, which my great friend Dave McKail, a Manchester rag n' bone man, had given me. Don't ask me why, but on the way back to Piccadilly, I had an altercation at a roundabout with a very aggressive van driver who tried to cut me up. The two of us circled the roundabout several times like matadors, me in my German helmet giving him V signs, which made him all the angrier. Eventually, we peeled off and went our separate ways. Next morning, I was summoned to Colin's office. He gave me the hairdryer look and I guessed a bollocking was in prospect.

Colin began, "I've had a very serious report that someone in a Piccadilly Radio vehicle has been seen dressed in a Nazi helmet and endangering a motorist in Bolton. I don't know who it was, but knowing you as I do, I'm certain there can be only one culprit."

I thought I was about to be sacked and spluttered my excuses about defending myself from a very aggressive van driver. Colin drew himself up to deliver his punishment. But as I cowered, an unexpected smile appeared on his face which then broadened to a laugh. "Get on with your work. And don't you ever bring the station's name into disrepute again." It was then that I understood that my 'crime' was just the kind of thing Colin might have done in in his early twenties. He quite enjoyed the anarchy of those early days at Piccadilly.

Finnegan was joined at Piccadilly by his colleague at Radio Nottingham, Stephen Beard. Their brief from Walters when they set up the Features Department was "to put Manchester into the heart of the radio station like words through a stick of rock."

As Roger remembers:

And this we loved to do. I was a Manchester lad brought up in Newton Heath, then in Fallowfield and I set about trying to investigate every cranny of the city to seek out any characters that we could turn into radio stars.

One of the best means of exploring the city was using the radio van which had a mighty pump-up aerial which allowed us to broadcast live from any part of the city. Often, we would just pick a major arterial road like Bury New Road or Hyde Road and trawl around looking for tempting little businesses or gathering places. I believe it was using this method that Stephen Beard discovered a quirky antique shop in Withington owned by an amazing storyteller called Abe Ginsberg, a former wrestler who was half of a tag team called the Black Diamonds. Abe had contacts all over Manchester - wrestlers, drag artists, musicians, and he became a regular contributor to the lunchtime magazine show, *Piccadilly Central*.

Then there was the wonderful Nobby Carr. Nobby was a man of the night who knew a lot of 'dodgy guys'. Blessed with a garrulous tongue, he was great value on air and spoke about Manchester with a familiarity which was authentic and always slightly underworld. Nobby was miraculously able to blag his way into virtually any club or bar.

On one of my radio car days when I was doing live inserts into the shows of Andy Peebles or Pete Reeves, I was cruising around the Victorian arches near the old Granada building, not far from Deansgate. Glancing through a gateway underneath an arch, I saw what looked like an extraordinary Aladdin's cave of gear. Clothes piled high in rows, old fridges, books, bits of metal pipe. I stopped the van and went into the archway. There were a couple of hand carts with big metal wheels, a pair of strange guys wearing odd clothes, long baggy shorts, and bobble hats. These were two of Manchester's last remaining rag 'n bone men and they were pretty hostile at first.

When their boss appeared from behind a bundle, he was of a different order. Dave McKail was an absolute gift to radio; cocky, funny, lovable in a flat cap. He told stories of the romance of the rag 'n bone trade, which was dying out, of wars over patches between the Salford and the Manchester rag 'n bone men, of the extraordinary and valuable finds he'd made when doing house clearances. Dave was an ex-paratrooper and amateur boxer, so his stories were legion and full of adventure. So McKail, like Ginsberg, became part of the woven fabric of Piccadilly Radio and they made regular appearances. It was a privilege to bring these characters to life for the city on the airwaves. And Greater Manchester was teeming with them if you looked into the caverns and crevices of this fabulous city. For a young reporter, I felt the same kind of excitement as a metal detectorist looking for Saxon treasure.

The beauty of radio in the late 70s/early 80s was that it was spontaneous. You didn't have to wait for an ad break or the top of the hour. If something was worth broadcasting, it was a case of 'Let's make it happen!'

Roger recalls a quiet day in the Features office, with not much going on in the Northwest worthy of editorial merit:

I was running out of options for interviews to play into the following day's music shows, when a small advert in the *Manchester Evening News* caught my eye. It basically said, 'We've invented the answer to every postman or delivery man's dream - a dog-bite proof suit'. This clearly was the answer to my dream.

Next day, equipped with a prototype of the suit, I drove out in the radio car to Platt Fields in Fallowfield. The Pete Reeves show broadcast a peculiarly sadistic request to the folk of south Manchester. "Take your most savage dogs to Platt Fields for the opportunity of a lifetime. Tear apart a radio presenter - Roger Finnigan. Go on, rip him to shreds!" And they came. As I struggled into the suit, a wire mesh undergarment with a grey polyester top, the beasts on leads arrived, slavering for a piece of flesh. "It will happen LIVE on air!" announced Pete … live on air.

Microphone in hand, I was to commentate or howl as the pack came in for the kill. Ethically questionable it might have been, but this blood sport, worse than *Fight Club*, would happen on daytime radio. The appetite the dog owners showed for this savagery was truly shocking. With shouts of, "Get stuck in Butch, give him some stick!" I felt the first jaws clamp on to my ankles and prepared myself for the worst … but amazingly, the worst I suffered was a bit of penetrative bruising. Had the suit done its work? Or maybe the bark of the pack was more ferocious than the bite?

Mark Radcliffe is another Piccadilly old boy who started as a producer and who is still broadcasting on Radio 2, as well as playing in a band, something he's always done in tandem with his radio career. His route into Piccadilly was another strange one as he recalls:

Piccadilly had come up with the idea of a short story competition and Colin Walters decided that the sack loads of stories needed sifting before the good ones were sent on to the panel of judges. He asked my dad, who had written a book entitled *The Piccadilly Story*, whether he could find a couple of students who could read the entries and weed out the dross.

As I was a literature student on summer vacation, it was clear that I was the man for the job. I recruited another student, the blond and beautiful Susan Nightingale, and we scanned the hoard of entries.

The experience, though, soon began to pall as entries ran into the thousands. And, even worse, Susan began to talk about her boyfriend a lot, something she hadn't mentioned when I offered her the gig!

One day when Susan wasn't there, I was really bored and so asked Colin if I could take a batch of stories home with me to read there. Colin said that was fine.

Off I trotted to the car park, where I put all the stories on the roof of my Ford Escort whilst I fumbled for my keys. I then drove away thinking, 'Blimey, there's a lot of wastepaper blowing about', before realising that I had driven off leaving all the stories on the roof of the car, so those poor buggers' entries never got a look in!

Anyway, that was how I first came to Piccadilly and then got the job with Tony Hawkins in the Drama and Classical Department (of 1!). The station's first venture into drama was with *The Last Rose of Summer*, a six-part science fiction serial which was nominated for a Whitbread Award. The 'department' would also produce *The Top Twenty*, a short series of dramas based around classic hits including *Another Brick in the Wall* and R. Dean Taylor's *Indiana Wants Me.'*

Brian Beech joined Piccadilly after two years as a teacher of English and Drama to eleven to eighteen-year-olds in Bolton. A speculative letter to Colin Walters saw him being appointed as a Road Safety Officer (a complete wheeze so that his salary would be paid out of secondary rental money). After three months, he was appointed sports producer, which included two Wembley finals with Manchester City ... difficult for a Manchester United fan. Next, he became a daytime producer, including eighteen months on the breakfast show with Pete Baker, which meant a 4am alarm call, sometimes not needed when he was just coming in after a night out in town. From programming to promotions and then from radio to PR:

My seven years at Piccadilly was the best time of my life. We used to go into work on our days off because that's where our family was. Best three memories? Playing football with Bobby Charlton and against George Best; producing and presenting an hour long special with Don McLean, 'A Slice of American Pie';

and winning a prestigious Sony Award for 'Best Educational Programme'.

Co-author Brian Beech with Britt Ekland, a meeting
she claimed in later years had never taken place.
(She's on the left ...)

John Clayton was originally appointed at Piccadilly as a broadcast assistant, before becoming Mike Sweeney and Dave Ward's producer. Born in Wigan, he won a scholarship to Oxford University (coincidentally to New College, where Anthony Blond, the co-founder of the station had been thrown out of a generation earlier) to study German, before paying his own way into the newly formed Broadcasting School where he excelled by producing a unique documentary on of all things ... silence. After ten years at Piccadilly, John would sell his soul and join the BBC, where he was Radio Lancashire's managing editor for twenty years.

Simon Cole joined Piccadilly Radio from BBC Radio Manchester and after a humble beginning as a daytime producer, became one of the most influential figures in broadcasting. His first start-up was the company that he founded with Tim Blackmore in 1989 with two staff and a single desk - Unique Broadcasting. They took Unique through much growth, many changes and 'quite a few mistakes', to emerge in 2014, through a reverse merger, as 7digital - a provider of B2B radio and music services in forty-two countries with offices in London, San Francisco, Copenhagen and Kiev.

His start at Piccadilly, though, was a little less impressive:

I had a particularly difficult moment in my first few weeks. I'd been given Phil Sayer's drivetime show to produce, in which we had a 'Schools Out' quiz for kids at about 4.15 every evening. On this particular occasion, I'd set the dangerous question as a tie breaker, "What's the capital of Germany?" This was before reunification and so the correct answer was Bonn, but I had mistakenly told Phil it was Berlin. The wrong kid won, the parents of the loser called in outrage, and we had to run the whole thing again. Just as I was sitting bereft in Master Control Room with my head in hands, who should walk in but Colin Walters - still Programme Controller at that stage.

"Are you producing today?" he asked.

"Yes," I replied sheepishly.
"Just so you know, we employ producers to make sure things like that don't happen - Okay?" he said calmly, just before leaving the room.

A lesson in management as well as geography.

Hazel Murray was a Piccadilly producer who went on to become the voice of the Flying Eye, reporting on traffic for Capital Radio through the evening rush hour, before becoming one of the best known of Sky TV's acclaimed team of weather forecasters. However, it was a hesitant start at Piccadilly as she recalls:

> I remember that Colin Walters did not think very highly of me, in fact he told me that I would never get anywhere in radio, as my voice was so poor. He also made me come to him every day with three new ideas for features. This was rather frightening, but nice to remember that half the station was trying to think up ideas for me, in particular, Tom Tyrell and Brian Clarke in the Sports office. I remember that a banana ripening factory was one of the ideas presented. Looking back on it, I realise that perhaps Colin was actually very kind, and had maybe seen something in me, but decided I needed a serious boot up the behind. Years later, he approached me as a presenter for some project he was involved with, but it didn't come to anything.

> Of course, for a few years when I worked a lot on air with Phil Sayer, many people thought we were having a torrid affair. We weren't. He always went on about my big bum, and when people met me for the first time, they often would comment that they assumed I had an enormous bottom and were surprised to find that I hadn't!

> One of my last memories of Piccadilly was when I got to do some overnight DJing – something I had no experience of whatsoever. A young man was paid to stand behind me all night and when I pushed the wrong button, he would push the right one. That was Andy Crane, who later went on to be famous as a children's TV presenter.

Crane had come into the station as a volunteer and after doing bits and bobs was offered a contract … at which point, his dad called Tony Ingham and asked if radio was a good career choice for his son, to be told that people were queueing up to join the station and this could be Andy's big chance. It was! He became a kids' TV presenter and is still working in broadcasting to this day.

Chapter 10

First with Innovation!

The best way to predict your future is to create it
— Abraham Lincoln, 16th President of the United States

It was 1981.

The first DeLorean DMC-12, later immortalised in the film *Back to the Future*, was produced in Northern Ireland.

The first London Marathon was held with seven thousand five hundred runners.

Bucks Fizz won the Eurovision song contest with *Making Your Mind Up*.

Ricky Villa's wonder goal won the FA Cup for Tottenham Hotspur against Manchester City.

John McEnroe launched a tirade at the umpire at Wimbledon, shouting, "You cannot be serious!"

An arrest in Toxteth, Liverpool, sparked nine days of rioting which spread to other towns and cities in England.

Serial killer Peter Sutcliffe was imprisoned for life.

The Centre for Disease Control and Prevention in the United States reported the first recognised cases of AIDS.

A massive worldwide television audience watched the wedding of Prince Charles and Lady Diana Spencer.

The first twenty-four-hour video music channel, MTV, was launched in the United States.

China became the first country to ever reach a population of one billion around the end of the year.

And Piccadilly Radio was broadcasting to a staggering one and a half million people across the Northwest.

***

Piccadilly was years ahead of its time in most aspects of its operation and nowhere more so than the promotions team, from duck racing to a daylong space invaders competition on the top floor of Lewis's department store. It even had the facility to listen to the radio station free down your telephone line … before premium phone lines were even thought of! You didn't need a radio to listen, you just dialled 261 on your landline.

In offices across the Northwest, listeners could pretend to be waiting to get through to 'Mary in accounts' but be listening to the station … which didn't make a penny from the service! It had ten thousand calls daily; twenty-two thousand calls on the day Princess Anne gave birth to the first Royal grandchild; eighteen thousand calls to learn about bus strikes; and twenty-thousand listeners tuned in for the snow line on road and school closures.

***

The excitement from a payphone dialling 261 and hearing the radio – even for the two seconds before money was needed (2p) and the thrill of having 2p to spend listening, which was rare. It made me feel so grown up at the phone after my Irish dancing class waiting to be collected by my dad. Then there's my mum waiting to hear the result of a competition when we should have been on the way to the dentist. She heard her name on the radio and that was so special for her. We had to run to the dentist, but she smiled all the way. It was a Joe Dolan LP with 'You're Such a Good-Looking Woman'. I was five and it is still so clear in my memory.
Maureen Fearon

***

The Bradshaws are one of the Northwest's best loved families and the exploits of Audrey and Alf are still listened to by thousands of people. Created by Buzz Hawkins, a comedian and a musician, he tells how the Bradshaws, set in a cosy terraced house with outside loo in the fictional Manchester suburb of Barnoldswick, came about:

In 1983, I began as a night beat musician on several shows, including one hosted by Gary Davies. Gary ran a weekly 'Poets' Corner' item featuring listeners' kitchen table scribblings. Unfortunately, one such scribbler got an unkind titter from the panel, and the phones lit up. We were challenged to write one ourselves.

Travelling home early that morning, I switched over from Piccadilly to Radio 2 and I heard Stanley Holloway's *Albert and the Lion*. Inspired, I wrote a monologue about a family trip to Blackpool - in rhyme and metre a la Marriott Edgar but using dialogue. The following night, I practised with some voices in the music library (Audrey's was the trickiest) and picked a slow brass band track for Gary to play under it. It went out, and once again the phones lit up - but in a friendly way.

We ran a new story once a week for a while and to my forever gratitude, Pete Johnson called me and asked me to be Overnight Producer.

"Producer? What do I do?" I asked.

"We'll give you the keys to the record library - just get what Gary asks for and bring your guitar as usual for your music bits."

Eventually, the shows caught the attention of the then programme controller, Simon Cole. He invited me to produce a new Phil Wood show in the mornings, which would feature the Bradshaws twice a week. For this, he kindly offered me five pounds per episode(!). I respectfully declined and suggested that I produce them for free, in return for front of house sales of Bradshaws' cassettes, and I would pay Piccadilly twenty per cent commission. We shook hands on that. Very soon, the Bradshaws' stories took off and they are still going strong today, over forty years on!

There used to be a few odd balls who somehow used to be always popping into the radio station. One such person was a young lad called Chris Sievey who was desperate to be a pop star. He would wander around the offices with a book binder containing rejection letters from every record label imaginable - which he was very proud of.

Eventually, he recorded and released a single with his band, The Freshies, which was called *I'm in love with the girl on the Manchester Virgin Megastore check out desk*. Of course, Piccadilly played it ... until the Radio Authority banned it because it was deemed as advertising. So Sievey re- recorded it as *I'm in love with the girl on a certain Manchester megastore check out desk*. Piccadilly played that too but, sadly, it only reached number fifty-four in the charts.

Giving up on a pop career, Chris put a peg on his nose, made a papier-mâché head and invented Frank Sidebottom, who made his broadcasting debut on a Saturday morning show. Radio Timperley was a ten-minute slot, with Frank supposedly broadcasting from his mother's garden shed. Chris was somewhat ahead of his time.

Way before internet dating, Piccadilly launched a Sunday evening show called *Making Friends* with John Mundy. Listeners wrote in looking for love and many successful matches were made, none more so than 'Janet and John'.

***

My wife and I both sent letters into 'Making Friends' hosted by John Mundy in the early 80s. I remember meeting a female spot welder from Altrincham and a snooty nurse from Salford who didn't appreciate my choice of a night out at Pembroke Halls in Walkden watching a comedian. Both were disasters, but it didn't stop me sending a letter to 'Janet from Wigan' and after three months and some disastrous dates herself, she rang me, and we arranged to meet on a wintry night in January 1982. We met and got on like we had always known each other and had so much in common we even put the same song on the pub jukebox. We had both been married before although we were only in our 20s so in no rush to get serious, but after three months I proposed, and Janet (Janice, actually!) accepted, and we have just celebrated our fortieth anniversary back in May of this year. I was going through some paperwork recently and came across the original letter I wrote to Janice back in 1981 using my middle name John.

So that's how 'Janet' and John met.

Alan John Hill

***

A minute past midnight – the first public
screening of *Grease* in the UK by Piccadilly Radio.

Chapter 11

When Radio Goes Wrong

*I like radio better than television, because if you
make a mistake on radio, they don't know.
You can make anything up on the radio
— Phil Rizzuto*

It was 1982.

Ozzy Osbourne bit the head off a bat on stage in Des Moines, Iowa.

Dark Side of the Moon by Pink Floyd had been in the charts for over four hundred weeks, around seven years.

The Doobie Brothers split up after twelve years.

Rod Stewart was mugged at gunpoint, and his fifty-thousand-dollar Porsche stolen.

Michael Jackson released the seminal album, *Thriller*.

The unemployed population in the UK rose above three million, the first time since the 1930s.

Argentine troops seized the Falkland Islands from Great Britain and a seventy-four-day war broke out.

Prince William was born. His full name was William Arthur Philip Louis.

The Hacienda nightclub opened in Manchester.

Also in Manchester, Johnny Marr and Morrissey formed the Smiths.

The Pope visited Heaton Park in Prestwich.

The Ford Sierra replaced the long-running Cortina causing controversy among Sierra-lovers.

And the Piccadilly Radio Marathon was held for the first time, with over ten thousand runners taking part.

***

Live radio was not without its potential disasters, but the 'seven seconds' delay' was always available to 'dump' what was being broadcast, to avoid the listener being subjected to some profanity or some sort of sexual titillation.

Phone-ins were part of Piccadilly's DNA – sport, medical, political, gardening, DIY. One evening, Tom Tyrell hosted a DIY phone-in.

"228 6262 for all your DIY queries. We're here until seven o'clock, so phone now. 228 6262."

In the master control room, a bored producer was putting calls through without much vetting. There was no need for the 'seven seconds' delay'. This was a DIY phone-in, so nothing contentious or controversial would be said.

"Okay, on the line I've got Jim from Wythenshawe. How can our DIY expert help you, Jim?" Tom asked.

"Well, it's this piece of wood, Tom," Jim replied.

"Okay and what is it about this piece of wood, Jim?" Tom asked again.

"I've got me dick stuck in it, Tom ..." came the reply.

Quarter to seven on a Tuesday night and some bloke in Wythenshawe has got his dick stuck in a piece of wood.

Obviously, every presenter had their own embarrassing 'live on air' moment. Mike Day, on the night Bing Crosby died, cued up the first track from Bing's *Greatest Hits* to put on after the news flash without checking what it was. *'Heaven, I'm in Heaven ...'* the old crooner intoned.

James H. Reeve played Queen's *Killer Queen* after the attempted shooting of Her Majesty at the trooping of the colour. He got the sack for that one.

Pete Baker was 'Mr. Dependable'. No matter what time he was on and no matter what was asked of him, he would never let anyone down. He was the ultimate broadcast professional. Other than one summer, when he was asked to fill in on someone else's show, as well as doing his own.

Pete picks up the story:

After a week of doing the Breakfast Show which had a 6am start, I was asked to fill in on Saturday afternoon for Steve England who was away. Being a weekend, the radio car was out and about at local events as part of the radio station's commitment to the local community. It was Susie Mathis's first time on air as a 'roving reporter' and she was at the Irlam Show, where there were a host of attractions, including a Festival of Motoring. I read out the cars on show perfectly, but then it came to the 'Car Stunt' display, where embarrassingly the 'C' and the 'St' got interchanged, live on the air. Unfortunately, we didn't have a seven second delay system in place for me to fade out or replace the offending item, so it was heard by listeners across the Northwest. Susie, ever the professional, said, "Well, nothing quite that exciting Pete, but there's definitely lots worth seeing!"

And a presenter, who didn't want to be named, wrote his own epitaph when he messed up the obituary tapes which were always ready in the event of a Royal death.

There were three different tapes, graded in importance of the deceased. The Queen and immediate family, priority one and so on. (Princess Alice - who no one had heard of - was number three.) When Lord Mountbatten was blown up at sea in Ireland, the poor presenter realised he wasn't included on any of the three lists but thought he should play something that wasn't 'poppy', so he played Acker Bilk's *Stranger on the Shore*, which, thereafter, became known as *Strange Bits on the Shore*.

Michael Gates now advises international companies on cross cultural negotiations as part of Oxford University, but for five years, he was a technical operator, the much maligned, but absolutely essential support for the smooth running of the station. His dad ran a garage in Altrincham and serviced Philip Birch's car. Like most dads do, he asked if his son could visit the station and perhaps get some work experience. He came for a week … and stayed for five years! It was only when researching this book that we learned that Mike's family emigrated from Vienna when he was six years old, and he recalls that he went to primary school in Rochdale dressed in lederhosen and speaking with an Austrian accent! Well of course, this all makes sense now … he was 'one of us'!

Gates tells a very good tale of his time at Piccadilly:

I don't remember the precise date my five-year radio career - if you can call it that – began. Sometime in autumn 1982, I think. But I know precisely when it ended. The stroke of midnight of New Year's Eve 1986. Officially, it dragged on into 1987, but New Year's Eve was the beginning of the end, as the green light flashed on the desk, indicating programme controller, Mike Briscoe, was on the line. I thought at the time, it should have been a red light, or a blue one, given the expletives that followed. And the red one showed the microphone was live.

The sorry sequence of events in the few seconds leading up to it were as follows … the tolling of Big Ben, Terry Wogan coming briefly on-air wishing Piccadilly listeners a Happy New Year from the BBC, followed by a blast of the Sex Pistols' *Never Mind the Bollocks*, instead of *Auld Lang Syne*.

I'd been listening - alone in the dark cocoon of a studio - to the infamous punk rockers as the boring party songs belted out for the audience, and – as usual – pressed the wrong button. I wasn't cut out for radio.

Mike had begged me – obviously as a last resort - to give up my New Year's Eve plans and do the programme leading up to 1987. "Just play the party playlist back-to-back all night, then wish everyone a Happy New Year. You can get a Big Ben sound effect from the record library."

But the library was locked, and nobody was willing to come in with the key. Jerry, the duty engineer, came up with the bright idea of feeding the BBC through the desk as "they'll definitely play Big Ben. But for God's sake remember to fade it out before Terry Wogan comes on."

Oh well … Humour was an important part of everyday life in the newsroom. Jane Beckwith drove to Agecroft Colliery to cover the miners' strike in a car emblazoned with the slogan, 'Nobody Does it Better'. Not surprisingly, it attracted unwanted attention, with Jane being greeted with a chorus of 'Get your tits out for the lads' from the miners on the picket line. You could hear it in the background when the bulletin went live.

Abigail Bonnell, then a rookie reporter, now a TV anchor in America, asked Trevor Green if he was interested in a story about a dead horse found in a ditch in Oldham and Trevor replying in his deadpan way, "Only if it's fucking Shergar!"

One member of the news team was a touch posher than your average journalist. He drove an E Type Jaguar and fancied himself as a bit of a James Bond … but will have to stay nameless for legal reasons. He had already blotted his copy book when he'd had to rush from the shower straight to read the news, without time to put any clothes on, but his best/worst moment came when he was on overnights with a junior reporter.

Bored, the journalist pre-recorded three news bulletins, all with slightly different running orders. He gave them to the rookie and said, "Okay, here's the ten o'clock, eleven o'clock and midnight bulletins'… and then shot off to the Press Club! The inevitable happened, a major story broke, and the absentee newshound was found out. No one can remember if he did the honourable thing and resigned or was fired … but he went.

As for Piccadilly Weather, that was reported by newsreaders sticking their head through a hole in the Piccadilly Radio branding going round the building. There was a door just before the news studio where they'd check whether it was raining just before going in to read the news – "Yes, it's raining," was the report, more often than not.

John Grey, the 'Memory Man', was one of the most popular guests on *Saturday Sport*. From 6pm to 7pm, listeners would phone in and test his encyclopaedic football knowledge. Players, games, scores, scorers – he knew the lot and was hardly ever stumped by any question. He remembered everything! On the Monday morning, after a particularly impressive performance on the Saturday, when he had answered forty-five questions correctly on the bounce, he rang the station the next day to say … he'd forgotten his coat.

Piccadilly was renowned for pushing the barriers and being quite innovative. For example, introducing the first 'Shock Jock' with James Stannage and his night-time phone-in. Colin Walters, with Stannage and his producer, would agree on a daily basis how many insults he could throw at listeners and get away with it.

The Radio Authority, though, had a robust way of ensuring stations did not overstep the mark. During the lifetime of the licence, a station would be allowed two warnings for breaches (effectively, two yellow cards). A third and your licence could be revoked.

James H. Reeve went too far for the Radio Authority by calling the Falklands task force, 'A boat load of psychopaths,' and a yellow card was shown (two meant real trouble). Subsequently, a memo went out calling for everyone to be alert and cautious when thinking of saying anything controversial or likely to break the rules. 'If in doubt check in first - on pain of death'.

Mark Radcliffe would go on to present the Radio 1 Breakfast Show with Marc 'Lard' Riley, but he cut his teeth at Piccadilly where he presented an alternative music programme. During this ground-breaking musical era, punk bands with titles such as Brent Ford and the Nylons, Dogs Die in Hot Cars and Half Man Half Biscuit were commonplace.

Mindful of the need to be cautious – 'on pain of death' - Mark rang Tony Ingham while he was on air and asked if he could play and mention a band called Throbbing Gristle. Ingham told him not to play it, but Radcliffe argued that he should, ''as it was a good tune.'' In the end, Radcliffe accepted Ingham's point but before hanging up said, ''I suppose the

Wanking Apostles are out of the question?" He did, however, play *Too Drunk to Fuck* by the Dead Kennedys, but bleeped out every "Fuck," which resulted effectively, in one continuous bleep.

Two of Piccadilly Radio's most famous alumni,
Mike Sweeney and Mark Radcliffe …
and three blokes from Chorlton.

Also, let's not forget the presenter who asked his guest how the new song was doing, only to be told, "Not very well, I've written a book." Or the producer who, live on air, said to Leo Sayer, "It must have given you a great deal of pleasure to write a song like *When I Need You*," only for Leo to say, "Not really, I didn't write it." Or the receptionist who when a band called Foreplay came in, phoned Mike Sweeney and said, "Mike, are you expecting Foreplay …?"

Chapter 12

Out and About in Piccadilly Land

*I remember when I was a snotty nosed little kid and Piccadilly
came to Warrington Town Centre and did a whole show
from the window of Dixons on a Saturday afternoon.
I'd never seen a rock star or been to a football match,
but I had seen the DJ I listened to in the mornings.
It was more than I could bear... I was hooked.*
— Chris Evans, 'It's Not What You Think'

It was 1983.

Singer and drummer of the Carpenters, Karen Carpenter, died, aged thirty-two.

105.9 million viewers watched the last ever episode of M*A*S*H. This was the most-watched finale of a TV show ever.

Manchester United beat Brighton & Hove Albion at Wembley in a replay to take the FA Cup.

Despite defeating Luxembourg in their qualifier game, England did not go through to the finals of the Euros.

Michael Jackson's video for *Thriller* was aired on MTV for the first time.

At Harefield Hospital in England, the first full heart and lung transplant was successfully carried out.

The Who announced the group was disbanding (for the first time) as Pete Townshend wanted to leave the band.

TV-am became the first ITV programme company broadcasting between 6am and 9.25am, seven days a week.

And Piccadilly Radio's Timmy Mallett was voted 'The Best Local DJ ' in the Smash Hit Awards.

***

Outside broadcasts, or OBs as they were affectionately known, were as exciting as they were challenging. If things had the potential to go wrong when broadcasting live from the studio, that was magnified a hundred times over when Piccadilly went on the road to record concerts, broadcast from summer fayres and shop windows or collate material for its award-winning documentaries and news bulletins.

Pete Johnson was an ever-present engineer on the radio station's OBs and he remembers the good, the bad and the downright daft:

> We had to go and record Mick Hucknall and the embryonic Simply Red early in their career at the International Club in south Manchester. Mike Winson and I went down some weeks before to meet the club's owner to check out parking and to see how we'd get the mic cables out to the recording truck.

> The club owner was Roger Eagle, a somewhat off-the-wall guy who promoted many good up and coming bands. The problem was how to get the cables out of the building. It had no opening windows or doors that we could get them through. There was a fire door near our truck – but no gap around it.

> "Hold on," says Roger and gets a brick hammer and bashes out two courses of bricks in the wall.

> "Will that do?" Very Basil Fawlty and the gig was awful.

OBs took place in the most unusual of locations … such as Strangeways Prison in Salford, when Tim Grundy broadcast his breakfast show from there.

As Pete again recalls:

> That was a technical and operational challenge if ever there was. I remember on the recce going round with a warder and him saying to us not to walk at the base of a wing outside. Why, because those dark blobs we were about to walk in were the shit

that the prisoners threw out of their cell windows above. He then showed us into the section with the gallows and trap door; all still there.

Roger Finnegan, meanwhile, had an idea to do a documentary about Bernard Manning and to include some actuality of Bernard working in his club, the Embassy. Instead of following him around with a mic all the time, we put a tiny clip mic on him and fed it into a small cassette recorder in his pocket. It got some great clips, but we didn't use the bit when Bernard went into the gents' toilets and didn't bother switching it off.

Live outside broadcasts took place from shops, retail centres, garages, schools, spring fairs – in fact, everywhere Piccadilly Radio listeners were!

Chapter 13

A Decade of Excellence

If work isn't fun, you're not playing on the right team
— Anon

It was 1984.

Apple's Macintosh computer went on sale, priced at two thousand five hundred dollars.

Michael Jackson experienced second degree burns from pyrotechnics while filming a Pepsi commercial.

Torvill and Dean entered the record books by scoring perfectly across the board, winning gold for ice skating.

British coal miners began 'the most bitter industrial dispute in British History'.

One day before his forty-fifth birthday, Marvin Gaye died, shot by his own father.

Comedian Tommy Cooper died live on TV from a massive heart attack. Some thought it was part of his act.

The Herreys' song *Diggi-Loo Diggi-Ley* won the Eurovision Song Contest for Sweden.

An assassination attempt on Prime Minister Margaret Thatcher and her British Cabinet in Brighton failed.

The Band Aid charity single *Do They Know It's Christmas?* went to the top of the UK Singles Chart.

Def Leppard drummer Rick Allen lost control of his car while driving. As a result, he lost his left arm.

And in 1984, Piccadilly Radio had to re-apply to extend broadcasting for a further ten years, as the initial ten-year licence came to an end.

***

Reapplication was a rigorous process preparing a detailed submission, which culminated in a formal interview before a panel of Radio Authority officers. It was taken very seriously and there was no room for complacency.

The station put together the senior management team who would answer the panel's questions and set up dummy scenarios with David Maker, MD of neighbour Red Rose Radio, putting them through their paces and asking probing questions. They rehearsed their answers diligently.

Come the day, the management team travelled to London and met up for a final time to rehearse the 'pitch'. They arrived at the Radio Authority's headquarters and were ushered into a room to face a panel of around ten senior Radio Authority figures. Their team was announced, then the Piccadilly team introduced themselves and waited for the grand inquisition.

The chair of the panel formally thanked them for attending the interview and for the detailed submission. He paused, smiled, and said, "Well, perhaps you should begin by explaining the secret of your success!"

The team weren't expecting that question and certainly hadn't rehearsed an answer. If they had, their response – most definitely - would have been "Philip Birch." These were the days before companies had 'Visions' and 'Values' or had 'Mission Statements' and/or a company ethos. An organisation took its personality from the person at the top and Piccadilly's secret of success was that Philip Birch had gathered together a team of young, hardworking people who were not only lucky and proud to work for the station, but understood instinctively what made it tick. Staff could rely on each other and were encouraged to try new ideas without fear of failure. Most importantly, they knew it was managed by a very astute and calm boss who backed them. Above all, it was fun and when work is fun, it's not work.

What actually followed the question was a very informal discussion about how the management team saw the station developing. Philip Birch confirmed that he would be retiring as MD and that Colin Walters would be replacing him. The chairman confirmed that the licence would be renewed, the only stipulation being that Colin would commit to serving at least three years to ensure continuity and stability and that was that! A bit of an anti-climax really but it was a great vote of confidence from the Radio Authority.

It had been a decade of excellence.

.

Chapter 14

Here, There, and Everywhere

Best bit of radio trivia ever. Guy rang me once when I was on breakfast on Key 103, told me in the final scene of 'Back to The Future', you can see two Piccadilly Radio car stickers in the window of the house next door. The house in Arleta, Los Angeles was owned by a guy from Manchester
— Steve Penk

It was 1985.

The first mobile phone call in Britain was made by Ernie Wise to Vodafone.

Born in the USA was released by Bruce Springsteen and peaked at number nine in the charts.

EastEnders premiered on the BBC.

In Britain, the National Union of Mineworkers ended a strike which had lasted fifty-one weeks.

Symbolics.com was registered, making it the first internet domain name.

Back to the Future was released. The film went on to become a cult classic.

Two Live Aid concerts took place simultaneously in London and Philadelphia.

Coca Cola changed its formula, releasing New Coke. The original formula was soon back on the market.

British Airtours Flight 28M, caught fire on take-off at Manchester Airport. Fifty-three people were killed.

And Piccadilly Radio hosted Manchester United's homecoming in Albert Square following their FA Cup final victory over Everton.

***

The iconic '261' car sticker.

The station was highly visible from day one and was promoted aggressively at every opportunity. As Chris Blackwell of Island Records said, 'If you don't promote, a terrible thing happens … nothing!' The iconic station logo appeared everywhere. Car stickers were phenomenally popular - at one point you could stand in central Manchester and one in four cars would have a sticker (more cars than listeners). Once that was exhausted, they became bedroom stickers!

Even now, the odd car, house or factory throughout the region can be seen with a Piccadilly Radio sticker. As Mancunian 1001 comments in his post *Your Music and Your Friend: 40 Reasons in Praise of Piccadilly Radio*, 'Most ubiquitous today remain the 1981 "Nobody Does It Better" stickers, with the earlier 1974 logo next numerous. Even more elusive is the sticker featuring the 1986 logo, with a fragmented '261' and

'Piccadilly Radio' on top using the Gill Sans typeface.' No doubt many readers still have a Piccadilly Radio sticker somewhere …

***

Hello from Australia!
Piccadilly Radio was so huge in my life growing up, I really can't remember life without it. The radio went on as soon as I woke up and if I could get away with it stayed on all day. I used to go to the New Century Hall Piccadilly disco which was amazing and made friends there for life. I also made a Piccadilly Radio stamp at school which I can still use to this day and I also have an original sticker stuck on my window here in Adelaide, Australia which gets many comments from lots of other POMS, who live over here. Those memories will be forever cherished along with the DJs who were just marvellous.
Kind regards.
Victoria Collinge

***

Promotions sourced t-shirts and sweatshirts from Portugal and selling merchandise was a roaring trade, so much so that the station considered opening a shop in the city centre. However, having no retail experience and the prohibitive cost of renting premises when it already had a city centre location, this idea didn't make sense.

One autumn, there was a severe problem with importing cotton and no orders could be placed for sweatshirts. The problem was solved by buying five hundred dark blue Russian army vests (from goodness knows where!) and printing them up. What should have been keeping the Russians warm on the Western front, were now the ideal Christmas present for Piccadilly listeners.

The Piccadilly Marathon was first held in 1982. Yet again, the station was first at doing different things … differently. The Bolton Marathon had been a massive success, but when the sponsor, Pony, pulled out, Piccadilly decided to organise its own event. Tom Tyrell was in charge, and he did a great job, aided by a bunch of helpers. It was the perfect example of when Promotions and Programming were in absolute harmony. Over ten thousand runners on the day and a prestigious Sony Gold Award for 'Best Outside Broadcast' were the result. Local firefighter, Kevin Best, won the race and then gave his solid gold winning medal to the Pat Seed Cancer Campaign ... so Piccadilly had another one made for him.

Mike Sweeney (left) and the late Tim Grundy (right),
two of the ten thousand people who ran the inaugural
Piccadilly Radio Marathon in 1982.

The station even got the legendary athlete, Ron Hill to head up 'The 4 Hour Club', with the promise that if you ran alongside Ron and at his pace, you would be guaranteed to break the magical four-hour time for a marathon. Ron and his fellow runners did it in three hours fifty-nine minutes and he said running at that pace was the hardest thing he had ever done. (His personal best was 2:09:28!) Ron had a camera round his neck and took pictures all the way round to keep himself occupied.

'Run with Ron'. The Piccadilly Radio Marathon
'4-Hour Club' with the legendary runner, Ron Hill.

After it had taken place, the marathon organisers wrote to the person in charge of the London Marathon, Chris Brasher, and suggested that the station could enter a Piccadilly team and report on the build-up, from the start and the highlights for local runners, talking to Mancunians on the run. Brasher literally scribbled on the back of the letter, words to the effect of, 'Who do you think you are? You should have entered in the proper way, rather than try and get in through the back door!' and posted it back. A month or so later, his PR team wrote and said they were inviting various radio stations to enter a team and report from the race talking to local runners and would Piccadilly like to take part! They got a phone call declining the offer and providing them with a less than favourable description of their boss.

Then, there was the Wombles Christmas Carol Concert in Piccadilly Gardens, which attracted so many people that the flower beds were trampled, and the daffs didn't come up the following spring. From the ridiculous to the sublime, as Pete Johnson mentioned previously, the station put the relatively unknown Simply Red – outside Manchester, at least – on in concert at the International Club in Rusholme. This was at the insistence of presenter, Tony the Greek, who screamed superlatives about Manchester's newest big act which he claimed was being ignored by Piccadilly.

Brian Beech, then as head of promotions, even gets a mention in rock journalist Mick Middles' biography of Mick Hucknall: 'The singer,' exclaimed Tony, 'has the best voice of anyone I have ever heard in the world.' Beech took up Tony's offer to listen to the new band in a vacant studio. "Hearing it," exclaimed Beech later, "I thought that Tony had undersold the singer. It was incredible."

Sadly, the concert was never broadcast as Hucknall claimed he had a sore throat, but after just one single, Hucknall attained icon status within the Manchester music scene. Beech went back to being head of stickers and t-shirts at Piccadilly.

The Bonfire Night at Barton Aerodrome attracted over eight thousand people and caused so much of a jam on the M62 that police forced the station to let everyone in free to clear the backlog. The car park couldn't cope and in the pitch black … well, we suspect people are still looking for their cars to this day!

Piccadilly presenters were real celebrities across the Northwest and thousands would turn out to see them. They would regularly switch on Christmas lights, not just in Albert Square in the city centre, but in town centres across Piccadilly Land. Piccadilly nights in clubs across the region featuring the DJs were the hottest tickets in town.

The 'Best Disco in Town' was very much part of the city's social calendar for under eighteens. It was held on Friday nights in New Century Hall and ran for two years, a massive night out with Piccadilly DJs, live bands and guest appearances from artistes, all for a one-pound entry fee. Kids queued from 5pm for a 7pm start and lots had to be turned away, but the canny ones used to find ways of getting in, giving money to doormen to let them in fire exits, storming the entrance, basically trying all kinds of tricks. So much so, that security had to be increased as the hall had a maximum fire capacity of seven hundred and fifty.

The Piccadilly Radio Fun Mobiles, the centrepiece of the summer Kids' Karnival and Funday Sundays.

A friend of a friend was told to sit at the rear fire exit, effectively the stage door, to stop people blagging their way in and to supervise the guest list. One night, a guy rocked up and said, "Hello I'm Pete Shelley. I'm expected." As he wasn't on any list, security, now used to all the blags, said, "Yeah and I'm Mickey Mouse, fuck off." The following Thursday, the guy says he nearly choked on his fish finger butty watching *Top of The Pops* when he recognised the lead singer of the Buzzcocks, live on the TV, as the person he'd refused entry to!

The Piccadilly Radio Fun Bus was always out and about across the Northwest, with hundreds of listeners turning up for a free sticker.

Presenters would open shops, car dealerships and take part in penalty shoot outs for charity in front of thousands of fans … who usually derided the presenter's lack of football skill. The Fun Bus would travel across the region giving out goodies or collecting for the Christmas Toy and Tin Appeal and the Kids' Karnival during the summer months became an important part of children's holidays, when teams of 'Whizz Kids' would travel to local parks and arrange activities for local kids.

The final scene of *Back to The Future*. Look closely and you can see two Piccadilly Radio car stickers in the windows of the house behind Michael J. Fox. The house in Arleta, Los Angeles was owned by a guy from Manchester.

The station was at the heart of all aspects of its listeners' lives, and it sponsored Manchester City versus Liverpool in the semi-final of the Milk Cup at Maine Road. National advertisers from London were invited to watch the game and Philip Birch asked Promotions to, "Think about something special to mark our involvement in the game." So, they came back with,

"Fireworks." If City scored, fireworks would be set off into the night sky over the Kippax Stand. (Again, Piccadilly was the first to do this.)

"Good idea," Birch said. "Let's do it!"

But first, the Promotions team needed to check if it would work. Could the fans see the fireworks over the stand? So, they asked Bernard Halford, the club secretary and a big friend of the station, if they could test a mortar, firing it from the Kippax car park.

"Of course you can boys," the very affable Halford replied.

So a pyrotechnic expert, Ron from Bolton, was sourced and the following week, the team turned up at the ground to give it a test, just as Bernard was locking up for the night.

"No problem," Bernard said. "Be my guest."

So, Ron went to the car park and set up his mortar. It was a blank as he didn't want to incur unnecessary costs and it would be enough to judge if it worked.

'BOOM!' Yep, that worked. And it was pretty loud in an empty stadium.

Ron packed up his gear and everyone piled in his car to get back to Piccadilly. As the team was leaving, they noticed a couple of police cars racing in the opposite direction. Then a police van was right behind them.

Tony Ingham was team leader on the day:

'I wonder if Bernard told anyone what we were doing?' I thought. As we turned into Portland Street, several police cars converged on us and an armed plain clothes policeman jumped on the bonnet and screamed at us, "Get out of the fucking car!"

We were all arrested, thrown into a police van and taken to Moss Side police station and charged under the Prevention of Terrorism Act. I tried to explain and Ron started crying, saying that he'd set fireworks off for the Queen. The police were unimpressed, and we were all thrown in a cell.

I asked to make a phone call. I call Colin Walters. "Colin you're not going to believe what's happened."

"Believe it? You've brought Manchester city centre to a fucking standstill. I've been asked to identify a car which stinks of gunpowder, and I've told them I've never seen it before in my life!"

It transpired that the IRA had left a bomb outside an army barracks earlier in the day. The firework idea was scrapped, City lost ... and failed to score anyway.

Chapter 15

Local Heroes, National Names ...

*Fame itself ... doesn't really afford you anything
more than a good seat in a restaurant*
— *David Bowie*

It was 1986.

The first group of musicians were inducted into the Rock and Roll Hall of Fame, including Elvis Presley.

The Challenger Space Shuttle exploded seventy-three seconds into its flight. All seven crew members were killed.

The world's worst nuclear disaster was the explosion of the fourth reactor at the Chernobyl nuclear power plant.

In the World Cup finals, Diego Maradona scored the 'Hand of God' goal and then 'The Goal of the Century' in the defeat of England.

Phantom of the Opera, written by Andrew Lloyd Webber, premiered in London.

British Prime Minister, Margaret Thatcher, opened the final stretch of the M25, London's orbital motorway.

In London, Prince Andrew, Duke of York, married Sarah Ferguson at Westminster Abbey.

Greater Manchester Police announced searches for the bodies of two missing children after Moors murderers, Ian Brady and Myra Hindley, made new confessions.

And Piccadilly Radio started broadcasts from the newly opened GMEX Centre; Alex Ferguson, the newly appointed manager of Manchester United, gave one of his first interviews to Piccadilly's sports team; and the station played *The Queen is Dead* by the Smiths for the first time.

***

Over the years, Piccadilly was a breeding ground for talent. It spawned a host of careers, both within and outside broadcasting, with many of the presenters becoming national household names.

Gary Davies is a lovely bloke and is remembered very fondly by all those who worked with him at Piccadilly. He is still presenting on national radio and television, not bad for someone who was once the resident DJ at Placemate 7, a Manchester nightclub.

Fun Boys Three - Dave Ward (left), Gary Davies (second left) and Phil Sayer (far right), with a 'lucky' competition winner at some sporting event … somewhere!

Tony Ingham was programme controller at the time Gary auditioned and he gave him some late-night shifts. The intention was to create an evening show aimed at teenagers to try and recreate what Radio Luxembourg and the pirate stations had meant to Piccadilly listeners of a certain age. Ingham thought that Gary could be the one to pull it off, but one day, Timmy Mallett - with the glasses and purple hair - literally burst into Ingham's office and said, 'Yayeee, I'm going to be a star!' One audition and then one Sunday afternoon show and Mallett was thrown on air … and the early evening figures started to soar.

A couple of weeks later, Gary went to see Ingham and said he understood what he was trying to do and agreed Timmy was the one:

"But where does that leave me?" he asked.

"Well you have to accept that this was the station's strongest ever line up," I replied. He wasn't going to replace anyone soon, so I told him he was the first on the subs' bench for holiday cover.

He said that didn't really suit his ambitions, so I said (genuinely), "Look that's my opinion, perhaps you should contact other stations who might have more opportunities."

A couple of weeks later, Gary asked, "Have you got a minute, Tony?"

"Sure, Gary. No problem," I replied.

"I've taken your advice," he said.

"What was that?" I said.

"To contact another radio station. I start on Radio 1 next week," he confirmed.

Gary was too nice to give me the finger to my face … but I bet he did behind my back!

So, *Timmy on the Tranny* exploded onto the scene, an early evening show for school kids and students. It was broadcast nightly from the fictional world of 'Timmy Towers' and the show was faster than a speeding bullet. The management soon realised that trying to control Timmy was akin to harnessing nuclear power … so they didn't bother. 'Just go for it, make it huge,' was the order of the day. And boy, did Timmy deliver!

Timmy knew exactly what young listeners wanted. We can all remember as kids when we first discovered the magic of radio, of listening to 'our' music with these cool presenters. That was the same magic that Timmy brought to a new generation of listeners. Chris Evans says:

> Timmy really was a genius. I still think about watching him work. He was truly insane, but for all the right reasons.

***

Gosh us fifty (cough, cough) plus girls were only laughing about this on Saturday and telling a younger friend about our star performance on Timmy Mallet's radio show! Back in 1984, four fourteen-year-old Stretford girls would regularly listen to Timmy Mallet's evening show. He'd often ask his listeners to ring in with a jingle ... so we put pen to paper and came up with a jingle to a speeded-up version of the 'Scotland the Brave' bagpipes song (no idea why, it just went with the words).

He loved it!!! So much so that he invited us in to sing it live on his show. We were supposed to stay an hour, but we had such a good time he had us make up and sing more jingles live on air! 'Radio Gaga' by Queen had just come out and I recall us singing to the chorus:

"All we hear is Radio Timmy, on the Tranny, Radio Timmy on the Tranny" (and repeat). He recorded another jingle which was played the next day during the breakfast show. This was midweek so we were famous on our school bus journey the next day. At the end of our live radio session with Timmy, he sent us off with his side kick to get some freebies, some stickers, and a white Michael Jackson glove (more like a glove you'd wear to test for dust in the house springs to mind!). The young chap was none other than Chris Evans, aka fondly referred to by Timmy as Nobby N'O'Level.

All four of us are still great friends and look back on this memory with fondness/embarrassment.

Lisa Green (and Fiona, Janet and Martha)

***

Timmy's helpers were just young kids when they became part of Timmy's crew. Some of them went on to slightly bigger and better things. Andy Bird became vice president of Disney; Professor Brian Cox used to make jingles for Timmy's show in his bedroom when he was a young boy; and Nick Robinson became one of the best-known presenters on the BBC.

Innumerable young people knocked on the door at Piccadilly Radio asking whether it could offer them some work experience and wherever possible, the station tried to accommodate them. One such individual was a young man from Macclesfield. He had already completed two weeks at BBC Radio Manchester, when they thanked him for his efforts and sent him on his way. That was how and why Nick Robinson made his way to the radio station at Piccadilly Plaza and asked if it could offer him a similar opportunity. Nick Robinson went on to become the BBC's political editor - one of the corporation's key journalistic roles - and a post he held for ten years. He is now a presenter on BBC Radio's flagship *Today* programme.

Nick recounted his stint at Piccadilly with much affection and gratitude in his book, *Nick Robinson: Live from Downing Street:*

> Curiously, I learned much more about journalism when I left BBC Radio Manchester and went to their local rival, Piccadilly Radio. I say curiously, because Piccadilly was renowned for its pop music output rather than its news. They were used to kids turning up who wanted to hand out stickers or dreamed of becoming DJs.
>
> When I arrived, I turned away from the studios and the stars and made a beeline for the newsroom. If I had turned the other way, I might have got to know another local kid, Chris Evans who, back in 1983, was helping the station's top DJ, Timmy Mallett. Our paths may have crossed briefly when I was invited to voice one of the characters on the *Timmy on the Tranny* show on which Evans, in the guise of 'Nobby N'O'Level, was a

regular. I remain proud to this day of my brief but pivotal role as 'Zak the Zit'.

In those days, even commercial pop stations had to produce locally generated news and current affairs in large quantities to hold on to their licences. Piccadilly had a three-hour nightly talk show with the grand title *The World from the Northwest*. The task of filling it fell to the presenter, Jim Hancock, his producer, Ian Walker, and for a few months, me. I might have been just out of school, but I was keen, I could talk to people, and above all, I came absolutely free. I'm not sure Piccadilly had ever come across a kid quite like me.

One week's work experience soon stretched into month after invaluable month of on-the-job journalistic training. Jim and Ian could have padded out their programme with phone-ins or blather about what was in the papers, but instead, they sent me off round the city streets armed with a UHER, the radio reporter's secret weapon - a portable recorder with clunky metal switches and chunky buttons and dials - and spools of brown recording tape to make mini-documentaries about Manchester's Irish community, Britain's road system and the 'changing face of the family'. I interviewed ministers, ambassadors, businessmen and lots of 'real people' as I soon learned they were patronisingly called by media types. The more interviews I could do the better, as the more time they would soak up.

When I listen to those reports now, my voice sounds unfamiliar, squeaky and self-consciously Mancunian and the questions so very, very earnest.

It could all have been so different. The world was indeed looking and listening to the Northwest … not, of course, to my worthy radio reports but to the music of Manchester.

Meanwhile, following a successful TV career, Timmy Mallett is now a much sought-after artist and marmalade maker.

The biggest product of the TOTT academy, however, was Chris Evans. He was a big fan of Piccadilly and describes it in his book, *It's Not What You Think* as …

> … a radio station where everything was groovier than anything that had been groovy before. Piccadilly Radio knew exactly who it was and what it was about. It was a new voice for a new generation. It was about the Northwest and everyone who lived there.

So great was Evans's desire to get into radio, he once followed Timmy Mallett home after an outside broadcast, but was thwarted when he got a puncture. Undaunted, he fixed it and went to the Piccadilly Plaza where the station was based. There, by chance, he saw Mallett leaving. "Hello Timmy, I'm sorry to bother you, but I was at the show today. I thought you were brill. I'm a big fan and … would it be possible for me to interview you before your show one night … er … for hospital radio?"

Chris didn't actually work for hospital radio. He didn't even own a tape recorder on which to carry out the interview, but Timmy said, "Sure, why not, come before the show tomorrow, we'll do it then."

> That's how it was that a goggle-eyed kid with thick glasses and the thickest, darkest, reddest hair, wearing a shiny white and turquoise jacket made his first entrance into Piccadilly Radio.

Evans describes how things progressed very quickly.

> The boss of Piccadilly Radio was a man called Tony Ingham. I phoned up to find out his name and immediately set about composing my note. I sent the letter to arrive before lunchtime on the Thursday and to my amazement and complete and utter joy, I received a reply from Mr. Ingham the same day. I went to see him on the Friday and started work on Timmy's show on the Monday. Incredible but one hundred per cent true.

And the rest, as they say, is history.

Mallett and Evans hit it off, with Mallett seeing the raw talent that Evans possessed. After one show, a brief conversation took place between the two of them:

"Er, yes hi, well done tonight, I would like you to think about a character for the show, something different, something you like, 'cos if you like it, the kids will like it. Something you can do night in, night out. Anything – it just has to be clever and funny, that's all." Mallett then paused before adding, "Oh and have it ready for tomorrow night. Byee!" and with that he was off.

Evans came up with 'Nobby N'O'Level'. Nobby had ten N'O'levels in nothing and his catchphrase was, "Well, what I don't know … I don't know." Nobby was an instant hit, and Evans was now an on-air personality. He started to be given warm up jobs for the various road shows and it wasn't long before he was appearing on the breakfast show as the tea boy, again as a character, rather than as a real person. This time he was called 'White and Two Sugars'.

One of Evans's closest friends at Piccadilly Radio was the aforementioned Michael Gates, a broadcasting assistant and an interesting character. He is now a high-flying business consultant, but remembers his time at the station, and his friendship with Evans, with great affection:

Nobby ended up living in a tent in my parents' garden, and even did an unannounced outside broadcast from there, which made the engineers as incandescent as their valves – until they saw he was actually in the studio playing a loop of birdsong in the background, having given out my mum's Bolton phone number as the call-in line, while I manned it. He was always supremely inventive. And, for accuracy, the story of him living in a tent in our garden hit the tabloids but wasn't one hundred percent true. It was too uncomfortable, so we shared my single bed – but top to tail, I hasten to add!

Gates remembers the time he and Evans once hired a video camera, back in 1987, to make a demo for TV stations. Looking back, Gates is sure that it was Evans's prototype for *The Big Breakfast:*

> Handheld wobbly shot of his alarm clock going off to start with, then Nobby waking up to a new day, speaking straight to camera about why he wanted to work in TV. Every day had always been a brand new one for him, full of opportunity. The final sequence was in his white Ford Escort and he turned to look at me and said, "Let's see what's on the radio, shall we?" I turned it on, and, right on cue, "There's No Business, Like Show Business" came on, and without skipping a beat he said, "There really is no business, like show business, is there?" A week later, I asked if he'd sent the tape off yet. He laughed and said, "Oh I forgot to lock my car in Manchester, and someone nicked it off the back seat."

The daft duo even came up with their own detective agency, 'Gambon and de Freitas'. The idea was to start it as a nightly comedy sketch on the graveyard shift, as a way of creating publicity for a real company with the same name. Gates wrote the scripts and Evans brought in a couple of friends to play the bad guys. "One of them is a real bank robber," he told Gates proudly. They got fan mail from Strangeways Prison. They even wrote a contract between the two of them, set up a bank account in Warrington, had cards printed (with Gates's mum's phone number), stationery, and even advertised in Country Life. They only got two calls – one from a lady asking them to follow her husband, but they were too expensive, and one from Andy Bird (a Timmy helper and later chairman of Disney International) fooling them into believing he was a high-powered American client. Gates still has the cards and stationery but gave the handwritten contract back to Evans a few years ago.

Timmy Mallett (centre) with his former helpers
– Chris Evans (left), aka Nobby N'O'Level and
Professor Brian Cox (right).

Stories are still told about 'the Geldof tape' and as ever with Chris, more than one person claims to have 'been there'. Gates most definitely was, as he recalls:

I suppose it must have been 1985, and Geldof agreed to do only one interview for commercial radio about Live Aid. Tim Grundy was dispatched to Malta with one of the new cassette recorders that had replaced the reel-to-reel UHERs. His brief, to record the interview and then Piccadilly would sell it to the network for, I think, forty thousand pounds. A lot of money back then. Tim handed me the tape on a Friday when he got back and asked me to transfer it to reel to reel, then edit it to the required length, a razor blade and sticky tape job in those days.

I was just leaving work, so I put it in my locker in the newsroom to work on over the weekend. What I hadn't thought of was that Nobby shared my locker, and it was unlocked. What could possibly go wrong? I came into work very early Saturday morning to find Nobby in great spirits. The presenter, for some reason, had put him live on air to talk about a boxing match he had been to. He had copied it onto a cassette from the slow-moving logging tape and was eager for me to listen to it.

As he produced the cassette, a sharp shaft of horror pierced my heart. It looked familiar. Yes, he had taken it from our locker he said cheerfully, blissfully unaware of the implications. I asked, "How long is it?"

"Oh, about three minutes." I gasped in relief. "But I was busy and just left the tape in."

"So, you recorded over the entire cassette," I inquired.

"Yes," he said and I burst into floods of tears. We both nearly lost our jobs at that stage. Fortunately, Mark Radcliffe weighed in with John Clayton (by that time deputy programme controller) who was rightly incandescent and saved us both, at least temporarily.

Evans was a genius, but that fact was missed by some people, most noticeably his new boss. When Evans was at Gates's grans, he held up a letter from the programme controller, Mike Briscoe, halving his salary. Gates recalls that you could see the light through the holes made by the full stops:

"He must have been REALLY angry when he typed that!" Evans said. Gates felt terrible as the reason was an announcement Evans made at a staff party, saying he hoped his mate took the station to the cleaners in an unfair dismissal case. Evans thought Briscoe was in the loo, but he was already coming up the stairs and heard it.

Evans's star rose very quickly ... and fell even more quickly and there is no one better to tell it than Evans himself:

No one tells you, "This is the day you are going to die." Furthermore, no one tells you that you're going to read a story about a little old lady ordering a birthday cake for her cat in the morning, talk about it on the radio and a few hours later, be out of work.

That is what happened to me. The cat in question was nineteen, which in human years, so the story claimed, was one hundred and thirty-three, apparently. I urged the cat world to revisit this generally accepted, but highly inaccurate formula, for converting cat years to human years and to please come up with a more realistic one. I then, for some stupid reason, added another line, which was so bad and unfunny, it still makes me cringe today:

"However, there is a good side to cats – there's the left-hand side, cooked medium rare with a garlic sauce."

After this last line, the switchboard lit up like a Christmas tree, but for all the wrong reasons. Never, ever mess with the emotions of owners and their pets. They are to be given the widest of all berths. The show finished at six o'clock and by five past, I was out of the door and out of work – silly, silly boy.

Chapter 16

Your Music and Your Friend

The power of radio is not that it speaks to millions,
but that it speaks intimately and privately
to each one of those millions
— Hallie Flanagan

Colin Walters came up with the phrase 'Your Music and Your Friend' and it summed up perfectly what the station meant to its listener. For the first time, they could hear music that was relevant to them, as well as new songs which weren't getting airtime on other stations. For example, with great support from the record companies, Andy Peebles presented the American Top 50 and as mentioned elsewhere, enjoyed great success with *Soul Train*. After Andy's departure, the baton was picked up by head of music, Mike Shaft, who could pick a hit, no problem.

In today's choice of highly formatted music stations, such an approach wouldn't work, but Piccadilly was of its time and simply played the music that the listener loved. And as well as the music, Piccadilly was also the listener's friend. The station was very accessible and highly visible. The city centre reception was welcoming and friendly. The presenters were always out and about across the Northwest, doing gigs, appearing at charity events, or broadcasting from the unlikeliest of locations.

Also, the Piccadilly presenters never referred to the 'listeners', only ever the 'listener'. Walters was very strong on telling the presenters that the magic of radio was that everybody listening thought that the presenter was talking exclusively to them. Susie Mathis and Phil Wood were particularly good at this, and one presenter taped a photograph of their loved one on the studio mic and imagined that he was just talking to her. The listener was valued, not tolerated. They were as much as part of

Piccadilly Radio as its staff. It was much, much more than just a radio station, it was a big part of everyone's daily life across the Northwest.

'Wood on the Wireless', hopelessly
devoted to Olivia Newton John.

As good a broadcaster as Sweeney was in his Piccadilly days – and he's still broadcasting to this day and still winning award after award – it was his connection to the listener that made every programme unique. Much of the material came from the listeners themselves and one of Sweeney's most popular features was when listeners called in with their most embarrassing stories. An air hostess once phoned in telling Mike that in the 1970s, she'd worked for an airline which flew Muslim pilgrims from Dubai to Mecca. For many pilgrims, this was the first time away from their village, let alone on a plane, so as she explained, boarding the plane before take-off could be chaotic. Some individuals would try to bring on goats, primus stoves and just didn't understand the need for safety:

It was really difficult persuading passengers to sit in the right seat. Many would be getting up and down before take-off, so we had to be quite forceful. As we were about to take off, one chap just wouldn't sit down, so I physically pushed him into his seat, strapped him in and told him in no uncertain terms not to move. About fifteen minutes after take-off, the man starts crying and it's at that point we realise he's an aircraft cleaner from Dubai!

Another time, 'Mavis' phones up, explaining that the previous Saturday morning, she was off to the shops, but the car wouldn't start. She tells her husband who says he thinks he knows what the problem is and will fix it, so Mavis walks to the shops. An hour later, she returns to see a pair of legs sticking out from underneath the car. Giggling to herself, she squeezes his crotch and runs into the house only to see her husband washing his hands at the sink.

"Who's that under the car?" she asked.

"The AA man," her husband replied. "I couldn't get it started!"

To make matters worse, the poor AA man was so startled he banged his head on the oil sump and knocked himself out.

One caller recalled in the 1960s being invited by his new girlfriend to Sunday lunch to meet what she described as her very strict parents. He was the first such boyfriend to be invited. After a very pleasant and formal lunch, the family gathered around an open fire for a chat, with all going well so far. The girl's father explained that every Sunday, they let the family budgie out of its cage and let it fly around the living room.

"So here I am in front of the fire, cross legged, when this budgie suddenly lands on my shoe which made me jump and uncross my legs ... and kick the beloved family pet into the open fire where it immediately combusted!"

Sweeney's *The Record You Fell in Love To* was also incredibly popular with listeners, with many tear-jerking stories of how music had been their first love. One day, a woman phoned in with a very sad tale of how she had fallen in love with a married man but had decided to end it after three years. Sweeney was as sympathetic as he could be and banged on about how even though they couldn't be together, she should remember the many magic memories they shared together.

"Did you stay friends?" Sweeney asked.

"No, no we didn't," the caller replied.

"Why, why not? You had something special, and he needs to know that. Phone him, tell him," Sweeney enthused.

"I can't," was the caller's quiet response.

"You were in love. Why not, why can't you?" Sweeney persisted.

"Because he's dead. He hanged himself in the garage last week."

Cue record …

***

Piccadilly 261 - WOW you make my heart sing. Growing up in the Northwest in Chester & Tiverton, 261 was my route to the outside world. It kept me in touch with the loves of my life, music and football. I was seventeen/eighteen in 1976/77. As I passed my driving test and could borrow mum's Renault 5, I used 261 to sign post me to what was going on and where. There were frequent competitions to win things. That night an Eddie & the Hot Rods EP & MC5 albums up for grabs. I won them all. I had to sit by the phone ready to dial. It paid off. Recorded it all so I could listen back. Can still hear me moving the radio and mic around as I moved to the phone & back – ha ha ha.

What times
Duncan Round

***

Epilogue

The Beginning of the End

What did I like most about Piccadilly Radio?
Simply everything, from turning the radio on first
thing in the morning. It was the greatest radio station,
anywhere. It will never be replaced and never will
there be a radio station like Piccadilly Radio.
What fantastic days they were!
— Frank Keelan, 'Piccadilly Radio – Pride of the North'

Since its launch in 1974, like all other commercial radio stations in the UK, Piccadilly had broadcast simultaneously on 97.0 FM and 1152 AM, or 261 metres medium wave in old money. It had been a resounding success and Piccadilly had grown to be the biggest mixed news and entertainment radio station outside London.

In early 1987, due to a nationwide reorganisation of the FM band, Piccadilly moved its FM frequency from 97.0 FM to 103 FM. A year later, the Government and the IBA began encouraging stations with multiple frequencies to provide split programming to increase listener choice and competition, advising them to 'use it or lose it'.

Faced with this challenge, changes were made quickly and dramatically. On 3 September, a brand-new station was launched, Key 103, (the name coming from a competition run for staff, won by the programme controller's wife). Positioning itself as 'Music! Not music' – the jingle being voiced by Middleton's Steve Coogan - Key 103 had a mix of rock and chart music and high-end specialist output. Piccadilly Radio, meanwhile, morphed into something completely different, Piccadilly Magic, broadcasting on medium wave, with a mix of older music and speech aimed at an older demographic.

That, though, wasn't the only change in the air. Having gone 'public' a few years earlier, Piccadilly Radio was owned by a diverse number of shareholders and a hostile bid to take over the company was launched by Trans World Communications, which had Owen Oyston as its chairman, who wanted to create the UK's first radio group.

Despite an aggressive defence by the board of directors, Trans World succeeded in gaining a sufficient shareholding to take control and the takeover went through. After fourteen years, Colin Walters and the board were replaced and, effectively, the halcyon days of Piccadilly Radio were over.

As the new regime moved in, many of the original Piccadilly team moved on, some to other radio stations; some to totally different careers. For them, a golden era had come to an end. But remarkably, after fifty years, the Piccadilly 'family' still exists. Every five years on the Saturday closest to 2 April, Liz Bracken, who was at the station on Day One, arranges a reunion.

It's not a grand affair, yet original members of staff from those early years travel from as far afield as Italy, Hong Kong, America, Canada and fancy London coming together to celebrate the fact that they were a part of something very, very special. A remarkable bond still exists that ties us together, even after half a century.

We can go for five years without contact but put us in a room together and there's an instant camaraderie. Sadly, the numbers are starting to dwindle, so it was important for us to tell this story. Many of the 'family' have contributed with their anecdotes (although some were far too rude to include, and some would have ended up with legal ramifications).

Outsiders looking in on the reunions will just see a room full of senior citizens in their sixties and seventies, reminiscing about the good old days; complaining that the music's too loud and the beer's too dear; comparing medical ailments; and sharing reading glasses to look at pictures of grandchildren.

But they'd be wrong. For one night only, we are all still in our twenties and thirties, having the best time of our lives catching up, remembering the way we were, proud to have played a part in creating a legendary radio station that we loved working for, and which was loved by over a million listeners across Greater Manchester.

***

I remember fondly the days of Piccadilly Radio in Manchester. Local radio played such an important role in our lives. It gave us our local travel and weather information. It gave local businesses the opportunity to advertise and reach a wider market. It informed us of major concerts and shows that were taking part in the Northwest. It made us feel 'connected' in a way that national radio could not deliver.

It also introduced us to some great presenters who were real characters with their own style. They became our friends and made us listeners feel special, as no one else outside the Northwest could hear how great they were. We would dance around the kitchen to new songs, then soon enough they'd be playing in the nightclubs and discos.

Writing these words whilst listening to these classic songs makes me want to hear this music again and again.

Stuart Littlewood

***

Queen summed it up in 1989 when the band sang, 'Those were the Days of our Lives'.

They really were.

Thanks for listening.

Acknowledgements

Thanks to everyone who contributed to the writing of this book, especially Henry Matthews for reminding us how Piccadilly was always 'First with News'.

The books that provided invaluable background information; *The Piccadilly Story* by Philip Radcliffe, *It's Not What You Think* by Chris Evans (HarperCollins UK), *Thank You for The Days* by Mark Radcliffe (Simon and Schuster), and *Live From Downing Street* by Nick Robinson (Transworld Publishers).

Our colleagues from Piccadilly Radio. This book is based on their memories and mis-memories, documented before we forget them all.

To John Clayton for being picture monitor and grammar checker.

To Pete Johnson, who appears to have combined his job as chief sound engineer with official Piccadilly Radio photographer.

(Sadly, hundreds of photographs taken by the official Piccadilly Radio photographer were set fire to by his wife in a messy divorce.)

To Mano at Cameron Wells PR for the cover design.

Also, thanks are due to the Facebook Group, 'Piccadilly Radio - Pride of the North'.

Thanks to Lionel Ross, the publisher and proprietor of i2i Publishing and to his senior editor, Mark Cripps.

And, most of all, thanks to Philip T. Birch, a broadcasting legend. RIP to a true genius and a real gentleman.

Fifty years.

Nobody did it better …

About the Authors

Brian Beech started his professional life as a teacher of English and Drama in Bolton. A chance meeting with DJ Roger Day prompted him to apply to Piccadilly Radio where he was appointed as a road safety officer by the programme controller, Colin Walters. (Don't ask.) In his seven years at Piccadilly, he worked as a researcher; a Sony Award winning producer; an occasional presenter; and head of promotional development, before a successful thirty-year career in PR. Brian has a BA Honours in English and American Literature from Warwick University and a MA in Creative Writing from the Open University.

Tony Ingham joined Piccadilly Radio as promotions manager, prior to the launch in February 1974. He spent eleven years at the station, becoming head of entertainment and eventually, programme controller. He also spent four years as programme controller at Radio City in Liverpool. During a twenty-five-year career in PR, he became involved with major regeneration schemes, including Manchester's Commonwealth Games bid, as well as the Lowry and the Imperial War Museum - North. Tony is now retired and lives in Saddleworth.

Contact details
piccadillyat50@gmail.com